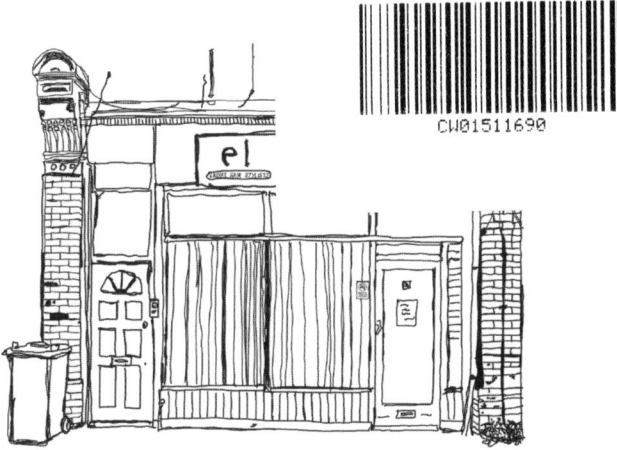

SPLIT ENDS

AND NEW BEGINNINGS

Olga Thompson

Synergy Publishing
Newberry, FL 32669
publishwithsynergy.com

Split Ends And New Beginnings
By Olga Thompson

Printed in the United Kingdom.
International Standard Book Number: ISBN 978-1-61036-912-1

Interior Layout Design:
Cris Convery
hello@crisconvery.com

Photo Credit:
Matt Canny Photography and Sharon Cooper Photography

DEDICATION

Stay gold, Ponyboy. Stay gold.
Johnny The Outsiders

For all the outsiders. For all those who have ever wanted to belong.

You are welcome here inside the covers of my little book.

Olga x

CONTENTS

PROLOGUE

Η αρχή είναι το ήμισυ του παντός.
The beginning is half of everything.

Take a seat and make yourself comfortable, let me take your coat, get you a gown and make you a cup of tea. This is my coming of age story, growing up in a little hairdressing salon tucked away in a back end street in North London in the 1980s. El Greco, the Cypriot Dynasty of Hornsey. A hidden jewel you could so easily have missed. A well-kept secret known only to others by word of mouth. The reputation of this tired, run down, unassuming little salon preceded it. Everything I am and everything I still ever hope to be, was born in this little hair salon. For all of life's blessings and battles, I keep coming back in my mind, again and again, to this little hair shop. My home, my place of worship, my anchor, my stage, my belonging. My beginning and my end. I want to share it with you too, all the enchanting stories spoken by beautiful women in rollers over steaming cups of tea, all the forever imprinted memories, all the wisdom, hope and counsel it has bestowed upon me.

Hair is everything to me, it was my first language. From the smatterings of peoples hair on the shop floor I would sweep up as a child, to the mountain of colourful worn rollers I would arrange into neat little piles on the rickety trolleys. It drew back its net curtains giving me my first exposure to the world. Hair shaped my identity, it consecrated my childhood and set me apart. Hair came to my aid when I needed it, strands hung like lifelines, pulling me out and upwards away from the things that both taunted and terrified me as a child. By day it filled my waking moments. At night coiled up in imaginary locks I dreamt of hair.

Hair is the first thing anyone notices about a person, that very first impression and often the lasting one too. Hair is the ultimate common denominator, we all share it to some degree: curly, auburn, straight, thick, fine, coarse, it both sets us apart and brings us all together. An invisible follicle cord that winds and turns enveloping us all. The marker for all the many stages of our lives. It both changes and evolves, sheds and rebirths as we do. It moves with us through life as we constantly shift and adapt to fit its ever-changing circumstances, jolts and wonders, sorrows and joy. We wear our hair like a suit of armour to embolden us to face the world. We can feel bereft and incomplete without it. Hair acts as a beacon of jubilant celebrations and a marker of heart-rending mournings, we wear it in so very many different ways

1

to mark so very many different occasions. The way I wore my hair swept up into exuberant curls for my wedding day is very different to the way it lay, straggled and wet on my shoulders as I gave birth in agony to each of my three sons. Hair evokes memories and voices, feelings of human touch, familiar smells and journeys we have taken. I shall never forget that pungent smell of Vosene shampoo being scrubbed aggressively into my hair as a child by my little Greek grandmother. Her rough hands kept me clamped down in position as my little defiant body cried and wriggled to get free in our chipped tin bathtub on Holloway Road. I hope when you read my story, that it will lead you back to your own memories and hair story too. I hope my split ends both make you laugh and move you, that they make you feel comforted and less alone in the world.

Everything I saw and experienced in this modest little salon with my little girl eyes both shaped me and made me the woman I am today. Hair clippings and smatterings of recollections that both defined my existence and etched a path for the way ahead. Hair was and forever will be my everything, the hidden cache of my existence.

So, come and take a seat under the dryer at this little North London hair palace for a moment. Sit back and enjoy the warmth and hum of the dryer in your ears and the glossy frayed Greek Movie Star magazine sitting on your lap, the air infused with hairspray and chatter, meatballs and cigarette smoke. Oh, and I nearly forgot to ask. Was it one lump or two?

1

ROOTS

Έφαγα τον κόσμο να σε βρω.
I ate the whole world to find you.

The fundamental basics of good hairdressing are always found at the roots. Hair follicles are structures within your skin that grow your hair. You're born with around 5 million hair follicles across your body. If you're Greek like me you can go ahead and double that figure. Knock yourself out, I'm covered in it. I am indeed 'hashtag blessed' with the furriest of downs. I'm such a lucky girl, it's genetics. I'm not joking, my uncle Nick is the hairiest bloke you've ever seen; hairy back, hairy ears, hairy fingers and a hairy tongue. Alright, maybe I made the tongue bit up to keep you reading, but you get the idea. I love playing the 'is it a ferret or is it my leg?' game with my husband in bed.

Anyway, imagine a hair follicle as a long tube that holds your hair. Your follicle is similar to a sock; so your hair is like your foot going into your sock. Love that. Just imagine going to the hairdresser and coming out with a new foot sock-do. No verrucas or bunions included. It would be an Instagram craze. Ultimately though, the roots are what it's all about. Origin and seed, genesis and crux. Its basic fundamentals. The roots are where it all begins. Let me take you back to mine.

Picture a tiny wide eyed 5ft Eleni Taliotou being introduced to a 6ft dark and striking Panayiotis Michael on the blazingly hot Nicosia steps in 1973 at her eldest sister's house, right under the Lemonia tree. My Mama said she remembered thinking how tall Baba was and also how handsome. However, he didn't eat the sweet almonds she offered him, which she took as a sign that he was uninterested. No sliding into your DMs back then to show you were into someone. He obviously did like her despite not sampling her wares; very much so, because he came calling back again the next day. He had quite a shock though when she opened the door this time as she didn't have her platform heels on, revealing her diminutive stature. Baba always lovingly joked to us that he had been tricked into marrying Mama, thinking she was much taller, because of her high heels. Baba was over 6ft tall compared to my Mama's tiny 5ft stature. Their families oversaw the courtship and were delighted at the match. During their short engagement Baba took Mama to

Famagusta so she could meet all his relatives and even bought her a bathing suit to go swimming. Mama, mortified, burst into tears as in all her sheltered years she had never been allowed to wear one before. It was an arranged marriage but happily they fell in love instantly. Their wedding was agreed and carried out quickly by their families, as was customary in those days. They got married on a scorching hot August in Mama's family farmyard in Paphos, with all the rabbits, goats and chickens in attendance. It was a happy day aside from the slight downer that all the wedding guests contracted food poisoning, due to everything being left out in the 40 degree heat.

My parents migrated to the UK before I was born, before the invasion of Cyprus in 1974. My Mama, a young bride, came to the UK not speaking a word of English. She fell pregnant with me when the war broke out back in Cyprus and deeply ached for her family and their safety back home. The longing and sorrow was so bad at times she told me how she would hold on to her belly and pray, worried that she would lose me from the inconsolable anguish. My parents escaped the war to forge a better life for us here in the UK. It wasn't easy for them and they really struggled to find ways to belong and build a life for us.

Their first rented flat in Shepherds Bush was run down, cramped and cold and was always leaking. Mama told me they were one of seven families sharing a toilet in their run down block. My Mama recalls that once, alarmingly, the ceiling caved in on them when she was eight months pregnant with me. Later, around the time of my birth they moved to rent a floor of a house in Holloway, North London.

I was born Olga Michael in Hammersmith Hospital in 1975. I was a red, screaming, angry baby having been sharply yanked out by emergency forceps delivery. This rude awakening catapulted me into the world and I simply wasn't ready. My birth certificate read the following:

As many of you as were baptised into Christ have clothed yourselves with Christ.

Gal 3:27-28 (ESV)

I was never sure why that scripture in particular was slapped onto my birth certificate, just beneath Baba's occupation: shoemaker. Looking back, I think this was a sign that God recognised that wailing, disgruntled baby and was watching out for her. I think He must have always had His eye on me from the very beginning. I was a puffy, noisy, restless baby girl, who refused to sleep. Baba would need to rock my cradle with his foot all night in order for me to settle, the second his foot came off I would start to scream again. Nobody was fooling me. I demanded round the clock vigilance. My parents stipulated that I tried to talk as soon as I left the womb. No surprises there I'm afraid, I haven't stopped gabbing since. My first word was at three months old apparently, my Mama can't remember what it was, but I like to imagine it was something fancy, a precursor to my glittering career like 'ring light' or 'support pants'.

In the year I was born, Britain was in the midst of a double-dip recession and tension, innovation and change were prevalent everywhere. The 70s were marked by new opportunities for men and women and an emphasis on freedom, equality and individuality, from the rise of feminism to punk rock. Britain was moving in a new direction, with many emerging aspects of modern life as we know it. *The Godfather Part II* won the award for best picture at the 47th annual Academy Awards and Bohemian Rhapsody topped the charts by Queen. *Thunderbolts of lightning, very very frightening.* Indeed, I don't know why but that video terrified me as a toddler. I think perhaps it was the white, stark chiselled faces popping out of the darkness like a horror film. I still can't watch it to this day. More importantly the hit Sitcom *Fawlty Towers* was broadcast that year for the first time on BBC2. It was our all-time family favourite show. We had every episode recorded on VHS and would never tire of watching reruns in the evening with big bowls of creamy steaming pastichio on our laps. Baba loved Mr Fawlty but I loved Manuel the clumsy Spanish waiter. He lit up the screen and made me laugh so much my tummy would hurt. Manuel was silly and funny and always dropping things. I remember thinking I wanted to be like him one day.

Back then a loaf of bread cost just 11p. Now it's like eleventy billion pounds. A pint of lager in a local pub was 20p, whilst cigarettes cost 20p for a pack of 20. I remember my Baba always buying his favourite Rothmans, he was never without a cigarette hanging out the side of his mouth. He managed to do almost everything with a cigarette; from driving his mini cab to mashing potatoes, it was a knack. We just needed to watch out for the fag ash droppings on our plates, which miraculously there never was. The average house price in Great Britain back then was just £16,980. Can you imagine? I think that's pretty much what I spent last week on a single pair of trainers for my kid. In 1975 Margaret Thatcher defeated Edward Heath in the Conservative Party leadership election to become the leader of the opposition and the party's first female leader. Her deep singsong throaty tone was the soundtrack of my childhood. I loved imitating her, with my Mama's oversized black purse which she reserved for church, slung over my arm. I never got over her taking my free milk away at school though and neither did my Baba.

My favourite photo is one where my Mama is holding me in her arms at one-years-old on Holloway Road. It was 1976, cue the psychedelic Egyptian wallpaper and lodged forever in my psyche, Tina Nymph, the famous woodland Goddess painting floating above our heads. The eyes of the voluptuous, kohl-eyed subject, painted in the saturated, sensual style of a B-movie seemed to follow me wherever I was in the room.

My Mama tells me I was born with such a thick mop of black hair and unusual blue eyes. I was always gutted that they never remained blue so as to set me apart from everyone else. No, alas I was resigned to having boring brown ones like every other Tom, Dick and Harry, or rather every Nick, Stavros and Georgina. My parents say as the first child I was truly spoiled. I take no responsibility for this, "as it was them who did the spoiling Your Honour". They were crazy about me and dressed me like a little doll with cute little outfits and matching shoes and hair clips. Another favourite photo features the "said" spoiled child in brown dungarees with an image of a red London bus splashed across the front. I had red hair bows and red matching shoes to go with it. I loved that little outfit. I wish it came in adult size now, I'd totally rock that look, nipping into my local Tescos for a pint of milk.

Though I spoke unusually early, I was extremely tardy at learning to walk. By 16 months I was still not walking like other babies, my Mama recalls. I suspect it was down to the fact that I was so well fed from all the chicken soup and dolmades pumped into me by my Grandmother, or Yiayia as I affectionately called her. Though my round ball shape may not have been conducive to walking, I was adored. My parents were the first of all their friends to have a baby and everyone lavished affection and doted on me. To this day, I'm not gonna lie, I do love me a bit of fuss.

There were so many photos of me in matching shoes and dresses. A plump, pampered and adored toddler. Snaps preserved from my Baba's Kodak camera captured me in my cot, in front of the television, holding balloons, in my bright yellow dress at my auntie's house, posing on the veranda on a hot Nicosia day in a blue and white flower printed pinafore, on my tricycle in our garden in the snow, in a knitted white cardi my Mama made for me. She loved dressing me up and my Baba loved photographing me. It's a travesty social media hadn't been around back then to capture every moment of my baby deliciousness. I mourn at the hashtags that could have been. So besotted were my parents that they even sent in a photo of me for a beautiful baby competition to the local newspaper, they were devastated that I didn't win. I wonder if it's too late for me to enter now? There's no way they could refuse a prize to a grown ass woman in London bus dungarees. Right?

Unfortunately, like most parents who obsessively photograph their first, this enthusiasm waned with the subsequent births of my brother and sister as the throes of busy family life took hold. Jokingly my siblings have never allowed our parents to live it down. I don't blame them when there are so many captures of the spoiled chubby princess and so few of them. I have this same dilemma with my three sons too. Pap away with the first, take a few photos of the second and then can barely remember what my third looks like; or even where I last left my phone (or child for that matter). I remember I even purchased a My Baby's First Yearbook which I religiously filled in for my first. I faithfully documented everything from his first tooth to a lock of his hair from his first hair cut. I saved everything, even… wait for it… his fingernail clippings in a tiny envelope (creepy much). As for sons two and three, I certainly do not love them any less, but I must confess, knee-deep in the throes of motherhood, the detailed documentation of their first taste of broccoli or the forensic analysis of the contents of their nappies, took a backseat. I'm pretty sure sons number two and three are relieved at this parenting oversight.

As it turned out, my parents' time at Holloway Road was a short one. One Good Friday, my Mama had been cleaning and left a turned on electric heater on the bed, causing a massive house fire. It was a traumatic event as my sister, who was asleep in her cot, was nearly lost in the fire. Damn you and your 'everything was made of cheesecloth and highly flammable' 1970s. My parents fled with us to safety but it was a hard period. It was difficult for them having two small children and sleeping on the floors of relatives', of relying on others and not having our own home. Mama tells me she wept so much during this time, that God must have heard her cry, because life suddenly and miraculously changed for us. Mama believed God had mercy on her and helped us to move out of the homes of our relatives, to buy our very first home.

So in 1979 we moved to Palmers Green, North London, or as it is more affectionately known "Palmers Greek". This may sound like an ethnic slur, but this long-held nickname for the North London zone of Palmers Green is actually pretty apt; the area is home to the largest population of Greek Cypriots outside Cyprus. Like many diasporas, the London community of Greek Cypriots, which spreads from Palmers Green into the suburbia of Southgate, Oakwood and Cockfosters, has its own set of rules, politics and social norms. It's like a little Cyprus saturated with Greek relatives and friends, shops and businesses. We moved into our new home when I was four years old, right before I started school.

To me, my Mama always looked like Aliki Vougiouglaki, the famous Greek cinema and theatre star we grew up watching on VHS tapes we rented from the local Greek City Video store on Green Lanes. I would love watching her romantic escapades on our little television with her on-again off-again co-star, the dark and handsome Dimitris Papamichael. Her flowing blonde locks were always blowing in the wind on speed boats or on top of mountains while she sang and danced. My dream was to be just like her one day. Like Aliki, my mama was always so relentlessly glamorous with her blonde hair, Cypriot gold jewellery and red lipstick. I adored Aliki but I adored my Mama even more. My Mama had a style and charisma about her that rivalled any silver screen star. She was my star. I rarely remember seeing my Mama without her hair done and lipstick on. She always worked full-time and struggled to raise my sister and I and then my brother too when he was born. I know it was hard for her and sometimes as a little girl I thought I'd see a wave of sadness wash across her face and then just like that, it was gone again. Like a wave hitting the shore and rolling back again before you can catch it. She was always dignified and controlled, always keeping herself poised, gathered together, never wanting us to see the pain and difficulty she went through to raise us.

My Mama made so many sacrifices for us to have a life here in the UK. She often retells stories to us of moments she felt alien and alone. It was an immense struggle for her not speaking a single word of English when she arrived here in the UK. She tells me how she felt very wide-eyed and innocent in this big new country. My Mama had been a hairdresser in Cyprus and my Baba, whose English was good, soon found her work in a little West End Hair Salon, right under the BT telecom tower, with a man called Sid. He was a hard man to work for and let's put it this way, wasn't the kindest to her. Once, a sheikh who came in asking for a perm from my mother produced a plastic bag full of money and offered to buy my mother for marriage. "No" she told him, shocked at his proposal, "I marry already". She recalled feeling terrified by so many new experiences and felt very lost. Coming from a tiny Cypriot village where she had grown up, she found life difficult here and she greatly missed her parents and ten siblings back home. She felt not so much as the immigrant she was but rather a stranger. Mama protected us from the sacrifices she had made for us. She was determined to shelter us from the painful experiences she had been exposed to. She had laid herself down so that her children could flourish and grow. Her greatest hope was for her children to have the opportunities she herself had not. She told me she felt anxious and awkward going into shops and trying to ask for things in her broken English. I saw how much my Mama struggled to raise us, taking us from childminder to childminder so that she could work. For the record I hated going to the childminders after school. I recall one lady in particular, called Margot. She had red hair, a stern face and gawky teenage children who never hid the fact that they resented us being there. I would often close my eyes there wishing the minutes and hours would pass faster. I'd open my eyes longing for the clock to miraculously jump from four to five o'clock. I longed for my Mama and waited by the window to see her after work. When I would catch a glimpse of her at the top of the street I would run out towards her. My Mama, beautiful, weary, always carrying bags spilling over with food.

The agony my Mama endured to bring me into this world visited me when I became a mother myself. When I gave birth I understood her and connected with her in a way I had never done before. The word mother rang in my ears in ways I had never heard or comprehended in the past; it clanged loudly in my soul, shaking my bones and wrenching me apart. Only now as a mother myself do I understand the sacrifices and the delight, the ache and ecstasy that birthing and raising children entails. I love in all-consuming, immeasurable ways I never knew I could. The same way in which my mother loved me all those years ago. A love that continues and never ends. Unfathomable, unbreakable. Becoming a mother gave me an admiration and respect for my own like never before.

My Baba began his career here in the UK working in a factory making ballet shoes. Sometimes he would bring old ballet shoe samples home and my sister and I would wear them around the house trying to dance like ballerinas, even though they were far too big for us, and despite tripping and falling all over the place, we persisted in our 'elegant' display. He would tell us stories of famous dancers who would come into the workshop for fittings, he had even met and made shoes for Ginger Rogers and Fred Astaire. He introduced us to their black and white movies, *Top Hat* was my favourite. The plots were always a little farcical and predictable featuring the leads always falling in a highly unlikely sort of love. But we were forgiving, as the plot always paled compared to the iconic duo's mesmerising costumes and dancing. I loved my Baba's stories and would ask him to repeat them to us again and again. It was my way of getting close to him.

My Baba struggled to fit in here. He allowed his name to be shortened and anglicised to Bob so he could get work. He even taught himself a Cockney accent so he could mix in with the other men at work in the factory. When we were a little older my Baba found work as a minicab driver. He drove the minicab on nights round North London to help make ends meet. He did that job till the day he died 19 years ago, but if life had been different for him he could have easily been a brilliant solicitor or even the most gifted actor. He had an intelligence and sharp wit that entertained all his friends. I remember he was always writing letters of complaints to big companies who he felt had done us dirty. From the dodgy freezer we were sold, to legal battles over parking, he was always fighting our corner. He hated the idea of injustice and wrote these long eloquent letters by hand. I think I definitely inherited this zeal of serving complaints from him, I too cannot bear injustice, I too relish writing long emails. To whom it may concern the owl themed novelty mug arrived in the wrong colour and now my LIFE IS COMPLETELY RUINED. PS ...your service SUCKS! Yeah, I'm one of those people. The other day my food shop delivery arrived with an array of fresh products which were expiring on that SAME DAY. Feeling the wrath of injustice and somewhat irksome and heavily menopausal, it dawned on me how "made for this" I was, I revelled in this auspicious moment and submitted a satisfying complaint to said supermarket on the phone. Don't get me started on the day I found a hair in my meal in a restaurant, that's a whole other book.

Baba's life wasn't easy as an immigrant to the UK. He had spent some of his childhood here briefly when his father had come over to search for work. While here, he suffered a traumatic car accident that saw him spend months in the hospital. His father wasn't around for much of his own childhood and he deeply struggled to show affection, but I knew he loved me, I felt it, and I adored him. Now that he has gone I love him in a new way. I understand him as a child and all his struggles and I love him for that lost little boy he once was.

My Baba had a great mind and a zany sense of humour and then later when he lost his hair, an eccentric love of his wig. I adored my Baba's wig. It was so jet black and shiny, fully theatrical, structured like a stiff elegant helmet. My most favourite times as a child were when he performed Elvis impersonations for us in the living room. My sister and I would scream "ELVIS! ELVIS!" He would love that and step up his rendition of Hounddog a notch all whilst balancing a fag on his lip and using the remote control as a microphone. He instilled in me such a deep love for Elvis. I'm still not sure if I loved Elvis just because my Baba did, the two merged over time, it was just another way to be close to him. He bought me a mirrored Elvis badge once that I wore day and night. I would even pin it to my pyjamas at bedtime, but annoyingly my mother would make me remove it before going to bed lest I accidentally and somewhat dramatically stabbed myself to death with it in my sleep.

I like to think he is watching me now from heaven and proud of his daughter telling his story now. His eccentric, chatty, funny daughter. I think that he would genuinely have loved what I'm doing now and have shown all my videos to his fellow cabbies at the depot. "Look at my daughter, she's a bloody nutcase, brilliant innit?". Baba was known as the minicab 'Greek Elvis' to his customers. He always looked like the actors in the Bollywood films he would rent for us to watch. He was handsome and had such dark skin and always wore flowery shirts to set off his jet black wig. As children we weren't supposed to tell anyone he didn't have his own hair. He felt ashamed by it and it was always kept as a top secret, but I never knew why. It made me sad that he tried to hide it. It was blaringly obvious he wore a wig and I bloody loved him for it.

To me watching my Baba was my first experience of theatre, it's where my deep love of wigs and characters began. He was an amazing impersonator and often spoke in funny voices when telling stories. Sometimes a man in a tight, grey, shiny suit and salt and pepper coiffed hair called Ken would visit our house with Baba's new wig in his briefcase. It was always a clandestine moment, like a scene from a movie. They would go up to the bedroom together for the fitting. We were never allowed to go up when Ken came and had to always play outside. I was fascinated by this event, the mystery, the secrecy, and longed to be a fly on the wall. To see what was happening of course, but more so also just to be closer to my Baba.

My parents didn't have much money, but had this knack of always managing to look like movie stars. I genuinely don't know how they did it. They always looked like they were going somewhere special even though they were headed nowhere at all. Life was gruelling and hard but they found dignity and grace in the everyday. They took hold of the mundane and they made it magical. My Mama always made sure my sister and I were dressed beautifully; whether that was crocheting our matching dresses herself or putting real flowers in our hair from the garden. Later when my brother was born they dressed him in funny little jacquard cream suits shot through with threads of gold. He looked so funny, rather like a full on miniature snooker player. Think of the '80s snooker legend Dennis Taylor, ok, now imagine him squashed. That was my brother. My roots, my upbringing, wasn't comfortable. Things were not handed to me easily. Like my parents, I worked, I strived, I struggled to take my place in the world and make sense of it. It felt like a battle from the very beginning.

I started school not being able to speak a single word of English as my paternal Yiayia raised me so my parents could work. I was very close to my Yiayia and I was given her name, Olga. She was a large, short woman with huge breasts, who too had known a lot of hardship in her life. My paternal grandfather had left to work overseas leaving her to raise her children on her own. She was a strong, steely woman who longed for me to love her more than I did my Mama. Whenever she would ask me I always told her that I loved my Mama more. She hated that.

Yiayia lived with us and I think that made the dynamics very hard for my parents, she always sided with my Baba and often made things difficult for my Mama. But we needed her help so my parents had to ride it through. To appease her I would be made to sleep with her at night, nestled against her giant creamy white bosom encased in her large white cotton gown, like a pillow. One of my earliest most terrifying memories is seeing her dentures like a floating smile in the glass of water on her nightstand.

As a young girl I would always visit Cyprus with my parents every summer. We always based ourselves at my maternal Grandmother's village Geroskipou, meaning ancient gardens. Yiayia Hambou was a sweet natured woman, simple and unaffected. Life's hardships had not hardened her like they did my paternal grandmother, rather they made her softer and more compassionate. Hambou was generous and delightful, like her name Charalambia meaning joy and light. I would love combing her long grey hair which tumbled all the way down to her feet every time she let out her plaits. She still lived on the original farm where she had raised my Mama and her 9 siblings and later where my parents married. The basic stone house lay untouched as the modern world encroached, it stood standalone and defiant as a motorway was built around it. The large primitive stone kitchen sink doubled up as a washing place for all the family. The toilet was a crude affair, little more than a wooden chair carcass without its seat, positioned over a hole in the ground, situated next to the goat pen. Terrified, I would hold my wee in as long as possible to save myself entering the hot smelly makeshift cubicle.

Whenever we were in Cyprus, we would visit the birthplace of Aphrodite and dip into the cool waters in the village. This is a huge tourist attraction, a small grotto, situated underneath an old fig tree, shaded from the warm Cyprus sun. Here water flows freely down a wall of rock and forms a pool amongst the moss. It is here, legend says, that Aphrodite would come to bathe, the waters are rumoured to be magical and transformative. According to Greek mythology, she met her lover Adonis at the pool, when he stopped for a drink while hunting. The meaning of the name Aphrodite is said to be "arisen from the foam", this is where us Greeks were 'gifted' the nickname "Bubble". It was commonly used in the UK during the eighties, I recall being called this many times in the playground, but you don't hear it so much now.

In Cyprus on the other hand, they called Greeks like myself visiting from the UK "Charliesas" meaning descendent of Prince Charles or Prince Charles groupies. I didn't much fancy the association with Charles or his big ears, so I think I would have preferred the term Bubble to be honest. I was aware of having a dual nationality, one foot in the UK and its brave new world, one foot in Cyprus, my grassroots heritage, my people and my home. Often I felt like I never really belonged to either, like a cultural misfit.

Aphrodite, who was adopted as one of the main Olympian Gods and Goddesses in Greek Mythology, was famous for great imperial feminine beauty with her constant smile, opulent jewellery and dresses. As her baths are situated in my Mama's hometown, as a young girl, I felt like this was a sign. I wanted to be like Aphrodite, with beauty that beguiled mortals and deities alike. Or at the very least, enough to just catch the eye of Christos Panayi, the cutest boy in school. As I dipped my hairy chubby legs into the pool, I prayed in earnest, full of hope, that the myth would come true; that whoever bathed in her waters would emerge beautiful and find love. "Please Aphrodite", I would whisper as I dipped my hairy stumpy leg into the cool water, "please let this happen to me; take away my moustache and fat hairy legs". However, when I ran to check myself later in the mirror back at my aunt's villa, disappointedly I still resembled Chewbacca. No one would ever notice me and not one single boy ever fancied me throughout school, well apart from Amik Shah that is, the boy with the bad milk breath. I never spoke to the Olympian Gods again after that.

For all of life's difficulties and hardships my roots have kept me humble and grounded. They have helped me to grow through painful seasons and arid spaces. As good roots give good growth to one's hair, so too my roots have sustained me through life's precarious and unpredictable roads, twists and turns.

No matter where you go, no matter how far you travel, the invisible thread of familial roots and belonging always pull you back to them. There were times in my life where I tried to push my heritage away to appear more 'English' to fit in at university with the other students. Later online I jostled my way through a crowded platform of funny English, middle class white women to try to be seen. I tried to be like them to fit in and to make myself more attractive to brands so they would want to work with me and to people so that they would follow me. I don't do that anymore, I always trust the right people will find me. I refuse to mould myself or to change. I'm Greek and I'm proud of the way I look, I'm protective over my history and of my humble beginnings. This is my story and I have given myself permission to live in it. My parents laboured to build a life in the UK and this made me the woman I am today. Where you begin is significant in life and though one has the power to change that there is still a primary residue, a fixed remnant that says this is where I began.

I've taught myself to lean into my roots and there I've found a wealth and richness of material. I think I've gotten 'Greekier and freakier' as I've gotten older. I've embraced my beginning and what my parents fought so hard to impart in me. I have come full circle to a place I call home. Sometimes you need to go back to the start in order to reach your end destination. Roots are wonderful, funny things and I'm proud to say that these are mine.

Knowing and acknowledging your roots is important; it reminds you of where you've come from and how far you still have to go. Roots are our anchor and our lifeline. No matter how far we go we are always connected to them, always tied to them by an infinite invisible thread. I am grateful for my parent's struggle and everything they went through. I am grateful that for so many years I knew what it felt like to be an outcast. Those difficult circumstances helped me to become strong, to grow, and find my faith and my voice.

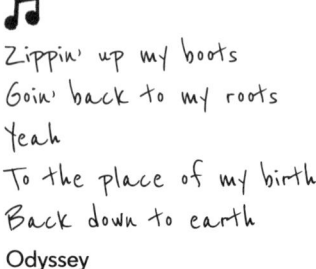

Zippin' up my boots
Goin' back to my roots
Yeah
To the place of my birth
Back down to earth
Odyssey

Always remember why you started. Sometimes roots can be difficult and we need to find a way to make peace with that. Honour your roots and your beginnings no matter how ordinary or insignificant you feel they are. Making peace with difficult beginnings can be food for the soul. It's human nature to look at what's not working in our lives, rather than celebrating how far we've come. When we take a moment to revisit WHY and where we began, then everything falls into place. Without its roots, a tree cannot grow. We can learn a variety of lessons about wisdom from trees. A tree with roots in the ground climbs to the sky. No matter how tall you have become, you should never lose sight of your origins and the place where you began. There is beauty and hope in our roots. Even if we feel our roots are shameful, or if people tell you that you came from a place of pain and hopelessness. Learn to celebrate the beauty of those difficult places, the adversity you overcame and the distance you travelled in spite of everything. That's magic. Carry that with you always.

2

WE ARE OPEN

Σπίτι μου, γλυκό μου σπίτι, γλυκιά μου καλύβα.
My home, my sweet home, my sweet hut.

Come with me as I pull back the net curtains of a little forgotten hairdressing salon. It's the summer of 1983 and Panayiotis and Eleni have earned the keys to their very own shop, it was a proud moment for our family. It was the very same year that breakfast television arrived on our screens and Margaret Thatcher the 'Milk Snatcher' (ain't never getting over it) won by a landslide in the general election. Wham! were riding high in the charts with Club Tropicana and Rara skirts were all the rage (mine was a peach one with bows on it if you're interested).

On that very first visit to the salon our parents took us with them, we were all jumping about with excitement. The salon door swung open onto a new cosmos for the Michael family. The place felt like a movie set! The vintage stand up hair dryers, the black onyx sinks, the hairdressing capes all hanging in a row like superheroes about to take off. I remember spinning round on the swivel chairs with pure ecstasy. This place was ours. It was exhilarating, like getting the keys to a new home. Mama was finally rid of her horrible old boss and was free to have something that she could call her own. Right there, wedged between George's chip shop and Singh's newsagent stood this little urban jewel of Weston Park, London. Tucked away on a little back street that one only knew by word of mouth. The story of El Greco had officially begun.

El Greco was like the TV show Dynasty, but set in Hornsey. We loved watching Dynasty as kids, following the mixed fortunes and perilous exploits of a wealthy Denver oil business family. In many ways the salon with all its goings on and stand out characters felt a bit like that. It was like the Buckingham Palace of hair. Growing up we thought we were Greek royalty or something. This grand residence was ours. Bright rollers, blue rinses and endless cups of coffee, a delicate balance of care and clutter. As a finishing touch my Mama displayed a variety of lovingly framed Dynasty stars and Lady Diana cut outs alongside posters of Vidal Sassoon couples with mousy hair in matching pastel tops, reclining nonchalantly on yachts. The air, filled with a familiar and comforting aroma of cigarette smoke and eggy perm lotion, combined with warm bread and beer shampoo. It was both nauseating and weirdly comforting.

A little shop bursting full of dreams and aspirations, those of my parents, the customers and even my very own. Everyone loved coming to El Greco; they could feel the bond of family love in that place. It felt more like a warm living room than a shop and we had let everyone in to be with us, to curl up on the sofa and feel at home. The word salon is actually French, originally meaning reception room. In 1800's France, the meaning grew to include a "gathering of elegant people" occurring regularly in such a room. That's what my Mama's salon was exactly, a place for people to gather and belong together.

Life at this vibrant '80s hairdressers was bustling. We had women and sometimes men coming in from all walks of life. Mr James the writer who looked like Father Christmas always came in for a haircut and beard trim, Toni the customer who never spoke to us but communicated in sharp grunts and came in at random times with her wheely shopper clad in a young boy's anorak that was far too small for her, to have her hair dyed pillar box red. El Greco wasn't just a hairdresser, it was so much more than that. It was a community centre where people gathered and a marketplace where Baba sold his friends factory outlet dresses out back. We had Avon ladies selling make up and tupperware parties here. Men selling sought after Encyclopaedias guaranteed to make your children smart and 'coffee readers' that studied your cup and told you the future. Often people would pop in just to have a coffee and a chat even when they didn't need their hair done. That's the kind of place it was.

At times it was a doctor's surgery, where customers would come and show my Mama their ailments and she would diagnose them all. I remember one customer asking my Mama to take a look at something down below that quote, unquote "looks like a pizza". Pulling down her elasticated joggers, the customer gestured for my mother to take a peek. My mother certainly did not have any medical training whatsoever but she was comforting and listened and made everyone feel better. If my mother was busy the customers took it upon themselves to muddle through and haphazardly diagnose one another "Oh don't worry Jean it's not a pimple I think you've got the bubonic plague, ah but four paracetamols and a tot of brandy will sort you out!"

One time, when I accidentally scalded my arm with boiling hot water whilst making tea for everyone, a Greek customer tried to fix me with one of her old wives tales by covering my burning angry arm with sugar and covering it in clingfilm. I was in agony, as of course the granules of sugar only aggravated my wound further. When they eventually got me to hospital, the A&E doctor said it was without a shadow of a doubt the most stupid thing he had ever seen. My poor Mama had been too polite in allowing her customer to share her outstanding medical prowess. Either way, I still have the scar to this day as a memory.

El Greco was also a restaurant. Everyone who ate there gave it five stars. Everyone got fed. From the customers to the postman who delivered our mail. No one would ever leave the shop hungry. My Mama would buy fresh bread every Saturday morning from the Greek bakery, along with sweet treats, halloumi loaf and small round baked buns perfectly dotted with black olives. She would often bring in our leftovers from the night before and lay them out on the little trolley for customers to help themselves. There was no having a bog standard custard cream with your coffee here. No, rather you would receive a side plate boasting a hunk of koulouri bread and last night's meatballs! That little trolley worked so hard, an all day heaving mass of meze on wheels. Mama was always cooking something on the back stove too, in the little kitchenette at the very back of the salon. There was always food everywhere growing up, we never had empty bellies and neither did anyone else who visited us. There was always something cooking at the shop or at home. There were always big pans of food left on the stove that my Mama had prepared the night before or the early morning before she went to work, so we would have something when we got in from school. I remember once being at university and receiving a Royal Mail delivery parcel. You might need to sit down for this if you aren't already. I opened the box to find, wait for it, a roasted chicken and potatoes. My mother was so worried about me not eating that she packaged up and posted this roast dinner to me. As touching as this gesture was, I must confess the chicken was ever so slightly sweaty from its travelling ordeal so I decided it was best not to eat it, but I loved her for doing that and must admit I exhibit the same behaviour with my own children. When my eldest son left home at 16 to pursue a football career I obsessed daily over what and if he had eaten. I didn't go as far as to post a roast chicken by Royal Mail, but I would be lying if I said I didn't consider it. Thankfully we have food delivery apps for that today. Mama was such a resourceful and capable woman, who was respected by everyone. Everyone loved Eleni. I vowed to be just like her when I grew up.

El Greco's was also very much like a busy zoo, often filled with a menagerie of animals. Customers would often bring their cats and dogs into the salon along with them. Everyone and everything was welcome. If you were having your hair done, then no question my Mama would cut your pet's hair for free. Now that's a deal you most certainly wouldn't get at a hairdresser today. I always loved it when Chinese Margaret came to visit us, with her parrot in a cage, all the way up to the shop on the bus from Kentish Town. I remember those days so fondly. He was such a bright, lively, colourful bird. I adored watching him beat his feathers, stick out his chest and squawk at us. My Mama always brought halloumi in on those days, as it was his favourite.

El Greco was a holy dwelling, a sacred space, like a place of worship that people would visit. My Mama was the holy saint helping and blessing all her customers with her beautiful worn hands. The Irish, the Jamaicans, the Indians, the Italians and the Greeks; they all came to this little North London hair palace. It was a place where everyone was made to feel heard and welcome. A house of prayer that people flocked to. People would tell my Mama their secrets and I would strain my ears to try to listen. She made everyone feel heard, she made everyone feel important. People would leave lighter, happier, as though time with my mother had alleviated their cares and absolved all their sins. This tired little hair salon transformed itself into a consecrated residence for people to come away from the world for a time and to leave again, renewed.

Mama would wake us up early on a Saturday to go to the shop, she would try desperately to find a way to mind us and still work. How she managed that, to this day I will never know.

My brother was a baby, so one of us would watch him in the cot in the back and the other would help out in front. We didn't have heating in the shop; it was always freezing. Mama had a clapped out old plug-in heater that she would wheel round to wherever she was working. It would take hours to get the shop warm, so in winter I never dared remove my coat. I could often see the misty cloud of my own breath on the glass mirrors. I remember Mama turning on all the big dryers to generate extra heat and thinking as a kid how they looked like huge astronaut helmets; I wondered if I wished hard enough that they would transport me somewhere, ideally somewhere that was heated. I would always use the little hairdryer to warm my fingers, then I'd do my brother's and my sister's too. The shop was fairly run down with its faded net curtains and damp, peeling walls, and nothing really seemed to work properly. Appliances were held together by masking tape to prolong their life and save my parents having to expend the cost and replace them. The boiler was noisy and unpredictable and had a tendency to pack up mid hair wash, running sporadically scalding hot or freezing cold water onto the poor unsuspecting customers heads. Getting your hair washed was like a game of Russian roulette. There wasn't even a door to the back of the shop, so Mama would hang up my Yiayia's old rag rug from Cyprus, hammered in with nails. I remember playing with it like a theatre curtain, imagining I was emerging from the wings onto a grand stage every time I came through with the teas and coffees. It gave *Stars In Their Eyes* vibes "Tonight Matthew I'm going to be...plucking Jean's beard!" Baba always said I was the more "professional one" who had a way with the ladies, as I am sure you can well imagine, I had all the chat. Soon I was promoted, I became the Saturday girl and my sister got dumped with my brother out back. I always preferred it this way, as being stuck in the back was mind-numbingly boring and also a tad creepy and the ceiling strip lights never worked. Save for the one high tiny slit window, the room was totally immersed in darkness. There wasn't anything to do back there other than stare at the hair towels hanging sadly up inside on makeshift washing lines to dry. My brother was boisterous and always misbehaving and trying to escape from his travel cot. As bad as I felt for my sister taking on the care of my brother, I was delighted to be relieved of my nannying duties, as I'm not sure how I managed it, but I always gave him the shits. I think God must have been laughing to himself at this point, knowing I would one day have three sons of my own. Maybe that was payback. I just didn't want to be anyone's babysitter! I wanted to be out front where the action and glamour was. I wanted to be right there with all the weird and wonderful characters. I wanted to know what Soulla was reading about her skinny cantankerous daughter-in-law in her coffee cup and why 86-year-old English Mary had fallen out with her 53-year-old Trinidadian toyboy. Out front I got to be with my Mama and my Mama's beautiful trainee hairdresser Androulla. Androulla was tall and beautiful and was blessed with incredible permed hair. Androulla was everything I ever wanted to be in life. She had a fiancé AND permed hair. I still go weak at the sound of her name to this day, *Androulla*. Oh, how it rolls off the tongue like a syrup drenched lokmade.

This happy, quirky London hair palace with its colourful ladies and men who would come in for their coffees, perms, George Michael highlights, gossips, sets and blow-drys, has never left me. It made me who I am today. An array of dazzling personalities sat in my Mama's chair, each with their own quintessential characteristics and mannerisms, bizarre foibles and habits. Women walked in believing that they would come out looking like (Baba's words) '50 quid!' That was a lot of money back then, a small fortune in fact. Baba always said that at El Greco anyone could become "a bloody movie star". I was ever hopeful that one day this could be me too. This little shop was my first experience of life and of theatre.

Wide-eyed I listened and absorbed all the people who came in through that shop door and drank in their stories; bottling them up inside of me for a later date. I was like a sponge taking in the hum of accents and clatter of mannerisms, a sprinkling of a thousand and one delightful quirks. Vivid memories of sparkling eyes and kind faces that will stay with me forever.

In a modern Britain in danger of becoming more divisive and less accepting, I want everyone to know the legacy of this joyful North London Hair salon and what it meant to me. It represents a time and space where people accepted one another. There are currently more displaced people across the world, than at any other time. People are being forced into unimaginable conditions, without food or water or vital medical aid. I am proud to be a supporter of UNHCR, the UN Refugee Agency which works to ensure that everybody has the right to seek asylum and find safe refuge, having fled violence, persecution or war at home. I do feel there is still a lot of suspicion and poor treatment of refugees in our country. Sadly the news reflects it regularly and that does not take into account what is happening locally, moments that would not be deemed newsworthy, but that are affecting the lives of so many.

A window into a vibrant post-1970s Britain, El Greco was a celebration of family and community. This was my community, my people and my world. I am grateful for everything my parents gave us and sacrificed for us. We had no idea how much hardship they faced because they made sure we never went without, but it was a struggle that did not pass me by. I could see how shop owners would mock my grandmother's accent when she would take me out with her. She was made to feel like an alien and often, I felt like one too. The post-war boom in immigration from Commonwealth countries was not welcomed by everyone. In many ways we felt like we were on probation, with our words and our behaviour. My parents' names were shortened and anglicised by people who couldn't pronounce them. My Baba's name was Panayiotis but they called him Bob. My Mama was Eleni but she became Helen. They didn't mind this shedding of their identity as they told us it was easier this way and would help them to fit in better.

Many times I was called a 'paki' for my dark skin and long hair, this happened many times to my parents too. El Greco became a hub and a protected place for all different nationalities. No one could be judged here as everyone was in the same position, many of us were here building homes and lives in the UK. All these outsiders, misfits coming together to belong in this underbelly of Hornsey life. The salon was a safe place, a place with no judgement. Within the refuge of the salon, people shared food, stories, songs and customs. A melting pot of cultures, a swarm of dialects reaching a crescendo, filling the space. Displaced people all placed together. People shared their fears and hopes, their worries and their prayers. It was tough for families like us trying to adapt to an outdated British system and British way of life.

Many of the customers who came to the shop were families like us who struggled to make a living. To support one another, we would often exchange goods for services instead of money. Nina would fix our shoes at her cobblers and in return my Mama did her hair. Someone else gave us tuition and my Mama in exchange would give her a perm as payment. I remember my Mama would get lots of Avon make-up products in return for doing the Avon Lady's hair. I adored thumbing through the polished catalogue, wide-eyed with little girl wonder at all the tempting, glossy items. Like goodies in a sweet shop. Avon secret wishes talc, St Tropez pink lipstick, Avon Ruby Raj earrings. People bartered and traded with one another in a currency only they mutually understood, and it worked. Watching my Mama I learnt about love and kindness. My Mama was accepting of everyone and they of her. At El Greco no one was left behind, everyone was welcomed. Here everyone belonged.

Sometimes I fear that my memory of this old little shop is fading. I worry that I can't quite remember the precise colours of the wigs on display or the exact hit in the back of the throat of the heady cocktail of cigarettes and hairspray. I fear it's eluding me fast, disappearing like a puff of smoke. Often my mother has said to me in her broken English "enough Olga with the shop, stop looking behind, look in front of you and your life now. Forget that bloody shop". But I tell her "Mama, this story is my life. Everything I am is because of it and because of you".

I just don't want to ever forget this place. I am so grateful to be able to capture the essence of it, its vibrant little beating heart, here within these pages. To harness those fleeting reflections and commit them eternally here to pen and paper. El Greco was my safe place, my very first stage, a place where I felt seen and heard. I saw my parents build something that was their own, which in turn inspired me to build something of my own one day too. That little girl who grew up watching her immigrant-Cypriot mother with broken English, work and sacrifice so much for her and her siblings, in a little hairdressing salon in North London in the 1980s decided to write a show all about this when she grew up. I wanted everyone to enter into El Greco, the Dynasty of Hornsey. This is why I wrote and developed my Edinburgh Fringe show El Greco of Hornsey where I revisited the salon through the eyes of my 13-year-old self.

I was blown away when my Edinburgh fringe show became a hit, El Greco of Hornsey received all four star acclaim. I think it was loved so deeply because it connected with others and their own memories and coming of age stories. El Greco was a celebration of a family and community with an enormous amount of heart. El Greco isn't just my own unique story, it represents the experiences of so many. It's a story of defying the odds and pursuing one's dreams. I will forever be deeply proud of this little stage show, this nostalgic little piece of '80s England. I was deeply proud and profoundly emotional to bring this heartwarming story to the stage. It was a love letter to my family, its past and present.

El Greco of Hornsey is a charming story with a nostalgic soundtrack and plenty of soul. If you're looking for a little piece of '80s England, traditional Greek hospitality and plenty of heart – this is the show for you.

Amy Macrae ****
Broadway Baby

There is nothing that a good cup of tea and a natter with a friend can't fix. Throw in a couple of custard creams (or a chunk of bread and halloumi a la El Greco) and we're rolling baby! We all need someone to talk to, to share our worries and concerns. I have always found that by being vulnerable it helps others to be vulnerable too. Verbalising your emotions can help lift a massive weight off your shoulders. Everyone is struggling, whether they show it or not. Bottling things up and trying to be strong can cause you to implode. Suppressing your feelings can lead to depression and anxiety. I know, I've been there. By sharing how you are feeling with people who are like-minded, you are heard and seen, you feel lighter and the load lifts. Surround yourself with good people that you can trust, lean into a community that you adore and makes you feel loved. We all want to "belong" to something bigger than ourselves. We crave relationships and feeling connected in some significant way to other people. It's important to both accept and embrace that. Everyone needs a place to call home.

3

OPERATION MULLET

Πιάσε ένα αυγό και ξύρισέ το.
Grab an egg and shave it.

Apart from the salon, Olga Michael just didn't fit, not anywhere. I was a short, plump girl with a monobrow and a funny sounding name. I resembled a chubby Glen Medeiros, complete with a faint top lip tash. It's worth a Google if you are fortunate enough to be too young to know who he is. Believe me you won't be disappointed.

I remember pulling my white socks up so high on the first day of school in order to hide my hairy legs. The socks had diamond cut out patterns so the hairs, coarse and defiant, would still forcibly peep out of the holes and taunt me. I clung to my Mama and screamed, calling out to her in Greek, red in the face, tears streaming down my cheeks, I just did not want her to leave me at this terrifying place called "school".

Mama tells me that I was always crying. I couldn't help it. I was just one of life's sensitive souls. I still remember the shock of watching the movie Bambi and sobbing into my flowery bedspread. There are millions of adults of my generation around the world who are still deeply traumatised by having to watch Bambi's mother die so bluntly. That movie emotionally scarred me. Disney set the bar for the most disturbing movie moments ever. I still haven't rewatched it to this day.

Birthdays were the worst for tears. I couldn't cope with the expectation and pressure to have this one perfect day just for myself. I would sob my heart out about something or another going wrong or even right for that matter. I would just get so overwhelmed with the birthday euphoria. I both loved and hated my birthday in equal measure. In truth, I still cry every year on my birthday. I want the attention, but the reality is I'm always overtaken with a deep Aristotelian woe that I am not worthy. I blame the birthday hype, it's so overrated, so much pressure to have a great time whilst looking at cards with giant numbers on them signalling how much closer you are to death. Cards with numbers on them are for children not flustered grown ass women with HRT gel dripping off their inner thighs, whilst simultaneously hovering over vats of meat on the

23

hot stove. We've all been there. Listen, if you're thinking about getting me a card with numbers on it then I'm afraid we can't be friends. Look, some of us take that sort of thing personally. Also none of this (and I wince) "fabulous over 40" on cards business either. Whoever invented those cards needs to be shot immediately. I hate the word fabulous. It suggests dangly earrings made by small children out of dried pasta and those dresses made from sofa fabric you buy in the back of magazine newspaper supplements. Nobody is ever allowed to say fabulous in my presence; unless you are Eddy and Patsy in Ab Fab of course.

Anyway, back to my moment of playground abandonment, "Mama don't leave me" I'd bawl in Greek, my beautifully plaited pigtails swinging furiously from side to side. The teacher who was trying to prise me off my Mama had a spine-chilling look about her, sort of witch-like. She had long dark red hair parted in the middle which gave the impression it was stuck to her head and always wore lime green tights. See, I told you – witchy. Her name was Mrs Ganiay but in my head I had renamed her Mrs Gangrene. I hated her because I was convinced she hated me. Most especially because she would smack my hands for continuing to play at the water table when it was time to stop. But I didn't understand her or any of the other teachers because I couldn't speak their language. She would say to my Mama "Please Mrs Michael please could you just speak to that child in English!" But of course my Mama couldn't. I was the daughter of immigrants, an unpopular kid who started school not knowing a single word of English. I didn't speak at school for the first two years, the teachers thought I was mute. I remember the school conducting countless assessments and hearing tests on me in order to get to the root of the problem. I could hear very well enough, thank you. I just couldn't get the words out. Greek was the first language I spoke, it was and always will be part of my psyche. It's what ruminates in my gut when I'm angry or upset. It is my mother tongue, from Ayia Marina, the first Greek nursery rhyme song that would soothe me to sleep, to my Yiayia shouting rough commands at me from the kitchen. Greek words and sounds punctuated my existence; big hot comforting soup of words that I drank in, filling my belly. A soul call of deep calling to deep. Greek was my first language, my first experience of finding meaning and making sense of the world, my passport to a rich, musical, ethnic world of my own.

From an early age there were signs that I struggled with anxiety and worry. I became obsessive about school, wanting to be the perfect student. I think it was my way of coping with the bullying I faced. If I was a top student the other kids couldn't hurt me. I would obsessively check and recheck my school books in my bag, tapping them over and over again with my fingers, counting them, like a ritual of remembrance to check that they were still there. I would also do this strange thing where I would often go to bed in my uniform ready for the next day. I wanted to be prepared, ready for any and every eventuality. I was always terrified of being late and getting into trouble. I became fixated on getting there on time, I would always force my mother to drop me so I could be the first one in the playground.

SEPTEMBER 1988

Dear Diary

Got a new school bag which says "I love tennis" on it. Thank you God. I'm going to look SO COOL. Also please can we get a Mr Frosty machine for Christmas.

As a child I was fixated on getting everything 'right'. I thought that if I didn't then something really bad would happen. I had a vulnerable assailable way about me. A 'please like me, I will do anything for your approval' demeanour. It's no surprise then, that I suffered traumatic bullying all through my schooling. I was physically and verbally abused daily by a group of girls who seemingly hated me and made my life miserable. Maybe I was just an easy target, I don't know. I was abhorred by them, my presence would either annoy them or be the centre of their cruel jokes. But the worst thing of all was the way they made me hate myself too.

It was most unfortunate that I happened to also share my name with the most popular school book at the time. Olga De Polga – the adventures of a Russian guinea pig. The kids at school revelled in making fun of me and comparing me to that fat overstuffed, furry creature. I mean you couldn't make it up. The timing of that was ever so unfortunate for me and not to mention a tad horrendous. That feral literary rodent has and always will be my nemesis. I would lie in bed and contemplate at night why my parents had named me Olga? For so long I hated my name and wished to be called something else.

I tried desperately at every opportunity to change my name but my parents wouldn't allow it. I begged and begged but to no avail. My Baba was horrified "Your grandmother, she turn in her grave that you don't want her name!" Nothing would make me change my mind. I was sure that if I had been called something like Lucy or Katy then I definitely wouldn't have gotten bullied and that my fuzzy limbs would magically have been born smooth! I tried to abbreviate my name, I even got everyone to call me Olgs, but in the end it just became Ogre which was also not hugely wonderful. That's it. I was stuck with my name and I hated it. It sounded ugly, just like me. Ugly and dumpy and stupid and fat. Of course Olga is a name you'd give a kid like that.

I always felt one step behind the other kids. The Cypriot outsider who never spoke because she didn't know how to. I began to loathe myself and tried to find ways to keep the bullies at bay by making them happy so they wouldn't pick on me. I had such low self-esteem and paranoia about my identity because of the names they called me. I can still hear those names today.

SHORT-ARSED. MONO-BROWED.
MISS PIGGY. CONCORDE NOSE.
FATTY BOOM. YOUR SANDWICHES STINK.
GREEK BUBBLE FAT FACE. YOUR GLASSES ARE UGLY.
YOU ARE UGLY. GREEK BUBBLE. OLGA DE VOLGA.
OLGA DE VULGAR. OLGA DE POLGA.

All I ever wanted was a cool-girl name like Claire or Lisa or Amanda or Kelly. That's what the cool girls were all called when I was growing up. I wanted a name that would make me belong with them and their long thin legs and swishy ponytails. All the boys ran after them during kiss chase. No one EVER ran after me. Who wants to kiss Miss Piggy with her chubby, hairy legs. Not even Edward the boy who always ate crayons and his own bogeys ever wanted to kiss me. Not that I would have even considered it. Even Miss Piggy has standards.

I like to imagine now that all these Claire's and Lisa's and Amanda's and Kelly's who seemed to be ever so cool to me growing up are now just really dull people with terrible haircuts, working on the reception desk of a concrete paving company. These are the same women with "Live. Laugh. Love." signs and crushed velvet diamante cushions in their homes. Payback is a sweet thing.

Oh yes, I had crushes, but they were never ever reciprocated. Christopher was an awkward looking and ridiculously tall young man, redeemed only by being the first boy at school to get an ear piercing. We slow danced once at my friend's birthday party. He was so tall I put my arms around his knees. He was kind to me and didn't look at me like I was a frog or a troll, so that was nice. I think he wanted to be a policeman and I couldn't see myself as a policeman's wife. I wasn't cut out for all those nights sitting in and watching Corrie on my own while he was out fighting baddies and cuffing Burglar Bills.

Engagement Mama and Baba July 74 Cyprus Paphos

Mama on her wedding day August 1974

Nobody dunk me. My
Godmother Stavroula and I
at my Christening July 1975

Mama and I Holloway Road
1975 September

Walk like an Egyptian wallpaper. Newborn with Baba February 1975

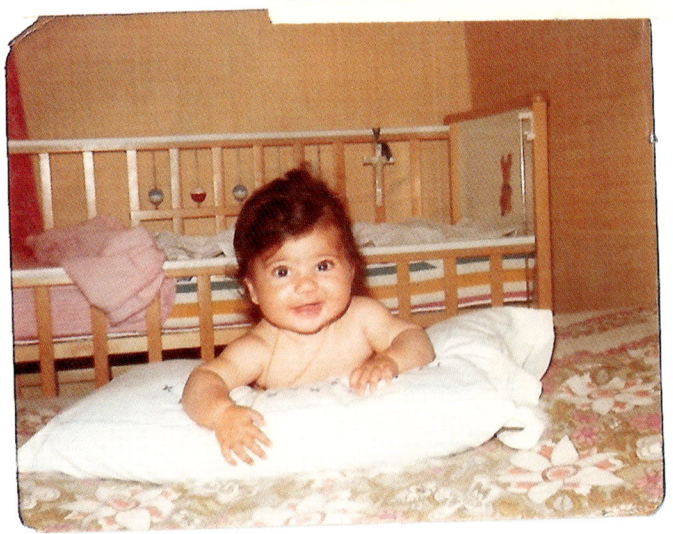

Hubba hubba. Holloway Road August 1975

Baba
and I.
Holloway
Road.
1976

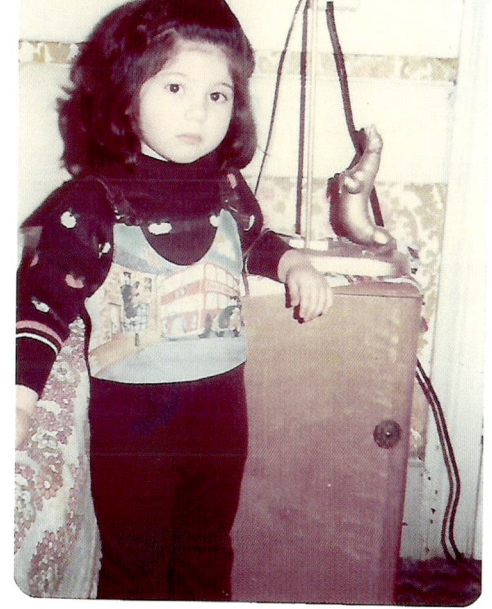

Dungaree love.
Holloway Road
1978

Lonely
goatherd.
Cyprus Paphos
August 1978

Outfit of the
day Holloway
Road 1978

Bath time
Holloway Road
1978

Nobody
touches
the cake.
Birthday
feb 1978

Christmas
Holloway Road.
1979

Mama and Baba rocking
the movie star look.
Palmers Green 1980

Starting Bowes school,
Arnos Grove 1980

Looking fly
with Baba
and my sister
Maria. South
London 1983

Greek dancing
by the bejam
freezer with
Yiayia 1982
Palmers Green

"Miss piggy" 1986

Operation Mullet 1987

Holding my newborn baby
brother. Palmers Green
January 1988

It's all about the banana clip.
Palmers Green 1991

18th Birthday birds nest hair
surprise. Palmers Green
1993

On the road with Riding
Lights Cornwall, 2000

Dressed like a
quality street.
Riding lights
2000 York

I will never forget the day I sneezed in class and a massive glob of snot came out. I didn't have time to catch it with a tissue so I caught it with my hand. I still have nightmares about this moment. Everyone looked at me with horror and disgust. I don't blame them, I just didn't have the kudos and finesse needed for a successful life at secondary school. They really should put that in the curriculum I think for all the uncool, socially awkward kids like me.

It wasn't just my name that caused issues, my weight also made me fodder for the bullies. I remember a boy lifting up my skirt when I was just 7 years old and calling all the kids over to laugh at my plump legs and tummy. I was mortified and wanted the classroom floor to swallow me up. Because everyone called me big I saw myself as big. I think for a long time, well into adulthood, I had body dysmorphia, always thinking myself bigger than my smaller frame. I wore myself like a costume never quite at home in my own body. I tried over the years to harness my body and bring it back home to me, but it kept eluding me and floating away like one of those balloons you lose at the fair as a child.

My grandmother would always pinch my nose in the bath with the warm water to smooth it as she thought it was too fat. She would tell me to belt my dresses to give me the waist I longed for. She would console me that even though I was tubby I had a pretty face. It didn't help. My family would affectionately say "Olga she has the puppy fat" as though calling it that would somehow soften its blow. It's how older generation Greeks of that time spoke I guess. They were always offering insults wrapped in sugar, "Oh she's got three chins and a lazy eye but let's look on the bright side, she has nice nails!" Don't worry about looking like the back end of a bus love, you just need a trowel of make-up, about the same amount they use on a deceased individual, a bit of soft lighting and no one will even notice.

I think in their minds they were trying to be kind, and offer me support, knowing that it was a stage that wouldn't last forever. But actually the term puppy fat is akin to being compared to an overweight canine. Ain't nobody wants to look like a dog.

After school I would come home and cry from the taunting about my appearance and weight, lying on my back with my legs up on the wall, because gravity always made them look slimmer this way. I loathed my fat body. I remember taking scissors to them and jabbing them imagining what it would be like to cut some of the flesh off.

Looking back I wasn't as ugly as I imagined myself to be growing up. Sure I carried a little extra weight but I can see I was a pretty child with big brown eyes and long eyelashes. I had lovely long thick hair too. I wasn't the girl everyone fancied or wanted to pin down in kiss-chase, but I wasn't E.T. either. Yet in my 8-year-old head, I felt like a monster, like my body was as big as our big brown living room sofa.

I think this struggle with my body image came to a head at drama school when I sadly allowed myself to get very thin in order to stand out like the other actresses. I would limit my meals in order to be skinny. Only now as I approach my fifties does my body finally feel like home. It's mine and nobody else's to comment on. I cherish its curves and scars. It's a miracle, truly. I like myself a whole lot more these days and I'm kinder to my body. I eat healthily and look after it but if I want the chocolate, then I have the damn chocolate. Also for the record I think Miss Piggy was fit. An icon in pink satin. She was a sexy badass and didn't care when Kermit rejected her. Looking back she was probably one of the first confident female characters on TV for many girls of my generation.

But alas I continued to go to great lengths throughout my school journey in order to fit in. I recall being so distraught at the possibility of everyone in Year 10 seeing my hairy stumps at the school disco that I managed to give myself a clandestine home leg wax with sellotape. My Baba's eyes twitched at the prospect of me having fuzz free jezebel limbs, so I did it behind his back. I think he thought my furry down acted as a deterrent against boys. Every Greek girl has the same message instilled in them by their Greek dad; boys = getting pregnant. Even a boy looking in your direction or, even worse, passing you a stapler in English could get you pregnant. We were told we had to be vigilant.

I'm not sure how logical that line of thinking is, as no boy would ever want to get near enough to me to impregnate me, unless it was pregnancy by osmosis. My Yiayia had already put the fear of God into me anyway, so I would have been terrified even if a boy dared to look in my direction (they didn't) let alone kiss me (they wouldn't). No boys were allowed for a nice, Greek, well-fed girl like Olga Michael.

Regardless of my family's well-meaning intentions, all I really wanted was for the other girls to like me and the boys to fancy me, but I was always at the bottom of the 'who do you want to go out with' list, notably always just above Sheena with the nits. In my dreams at night though, I was number one. In my indulgent slumber I had a long swishy ponytail and elongated smooth limbs like Claire and her groupies and George Michael (pre his revelation, of course) naturally wanted to date me. I vividly remember the dream scenario to this day, it was always the same one. I'd be at a Wham! concert looking delectable (understandably) in a gold puffball dress and gold banana clip.

George Michael would be gyrating and singing on stage and he would suddenly spot me in the crowd. Gasp. Having laid eyes on me he would now justifiably struggle to concentrate, stumbling over his lyrics, tripping over his dance moves, mesmerised by my exquisiteness, the sheer volume of fabric on my dress and possibly my monobrow. Later he would send one of his bodyguards out to look for me and bring me back to his dressing room. "George has requested to meet with you," they would say. I would look taken aback and shocked as my girlfriends, though bitterly disappointed it had not been one of them, would manage to clap, whoop and cheer that I had been the chosen one. Finally when George had me and all my puffball glory to himself, he would ask me if he could visit my parents in Palmers Green to request their permission to take me on a date to McDonald's. In hindsight I wish I'd chosen somewhere fancier for George to take me in my dream. I mean surely the guy could afford it and I in my gold puffball dress avec monobrow and matching shoes was most definitely worth it. My outfit was worthy of at least a Wimpy for sure. FYI In my dreams I was called Lisa, or Demi, or Suzi and definitely not Olga. George would never date an Olga.

DECEMBER 1987

Dear Diary

Please help me to look even better than last year. It would be great if my moustache stopped growing. Also if God reads this I want to marry George Michael and have his babies.

There were of course, happy times too growing up. The summer of 1984 when my Yiayia and Papou had travelled from Cyprus to stay with us at our house in London. I loved it when they came to visit. I was nine and remember thinking it was the best time of my entire life. It was a hot summer's evening and my Mama was doing souvlakia in the garden on the barbecue. We were dancing to Greek music on the cassette player in the kitchen. My Yiayia would stand next to our fancy bejam fridge freezer and clap and say "Bravo Olga" and shower me with ten pound notes. I remember feeling so happy and laughing so much that my cheeks were bursting! I was so relaxed and carefree because it was the summer holidays and we didn't have to go to school. I really didn't like school, I was terrified of it. School holidays gave me respite from the taunting, they were my safe place. That summer right there in that little pine walled kitchen in Palmers Green, I was enjoying one of the happiest moments of my childhood.

I taught myself to survive my childhood by making everybody laugh. As long as I entertained the kids at school then they wouldn't pick on me. Comedy became a shield for me, a secret weapon I could use against their spitefulness and jeers. I got clever at mocking and devaluing myself before they could. The spitting and hitting and pushing damaged my confidence. I loathed myself. I would come home after school and scream into my pillow. Mother Nature may have made me fat, but I decided to get my own back on her by being funny. Funny became my thing and I worked hard at it and became good at it. It was great to have something that was mine and mine alone, something that was in my control. No one could take it away from me. I'd make up jokes and character names in my head. When I couldn't sleep at night I'd imagine a TV show playing where I was the star who made people laugh.

My Mama saw my lack of self confidence and did all she could to build me up. Bleaching my hairy sideburns, plucking my monobrow, waxing my moustache and yes, oh yes, cutting me the sharpest of mullets. Which unfortunately, as previously mentioned, only served to make me look like a male '80s new romantic singer. Have you Googled him yet? My Mama's broken English meant she was unable to articulately fight for me at school. She didn't have the words, the language. So she fought for me the only way she knew how… with her scissors. She taught me to stand up tall and make the best of myself. She would say "Olga always put your lipstick on, a woman with no lipstick on is like a plain potato." Listen nobody and I mean nobody wants to look like a potato, least of all me.

I have told my story so many times. Over and over again about how being bullied as a child shaped me to be who I am today. I've been told to shut up and "Get over it snowflake" online. It doesn't bother me too much, my skin is a lot tougher than what it used to be. Also I've been called far worse than that online over the years. But let me tell you something for reference; you don't get beaten up in a girls school toilet and just forget about it. Some days I can still feel like that short, monobrowed chubby kid with the odd sounding name. "Snowflake" is used negatively; it has a connotation of being inherently wet or fragile. But, do you know what, I'm proud to be a snowflake. I actually think that these small crystal facets scattering sunlight with their unique and complex designs are actually rather beautiful. Did you know as snowflakes tumble through the air, swirling and spiralling, they each take a different path to the ground. This course shapes each snowflake differently. Just like us as people and the way life knocks, throws and alters us. Each snowflake is fully formed, unique and special just like you and me. I hope I will never stop sharing my experiences and my journey in order that I might help others. For some of us, trauma fractures us forever, but in such a way that we become more inherently beautiful because of it.

I'm always asked if I brought the bullies to account, if I ever made them pay for what they did. The answer is no. Nor would I want to. Recently one of them found me on social media and tried to befriend me. I wasn't unkind. I have forgiven them, after all they were only children themselves. However, that doesn't mean I want to be friends. I really don't. I'm careful about who I let in these days. I protect my peace at all costs. I'm smarter and more intuitive. I have learnt to safeguard little Olga, because despite the narrative she was told, little Olga was really pretty special. I was the underdog, the one they underestimated and looked at like I was something on the bottom of their shoe. I defied every single one of their expectations. I'm glad I didn't fit in with them, because look at me now.

I have chosen to forgive people and situations in my life that nearly destroyed me. Why? Well, truthfully I did it for me, not them. I didn't want to carry that bile around in my body anymore. By forgiving the bullies I was free from my tie to the wrong they had caused me. I don't ever want to sacrifice my peace. It doesn't make what happened ok but it makes me feel ok, if that makes any sense? I find that when I make the decision to truly forgive, then the will and desire follows. Holding grudges can mentally wear you out and make you miserable. They took enough from me. I'm not giving them my hate and bitterness too.

It was everything that was right about me, that made me stick out as a child. It's time for me to celebrate who I was. I see now, there was never anything wrong with Olga Michael.

Never worry about being the misfit, the one who is misunderstood, the under-dog. You are special and set apart, unique, why would you want to be like everyone else? Let people underestimate you, refuse to fit in their boxes, you are bigger than that and you certainly don't need their approval. You may feel like you have the odds stacked against you but you keep on showing up and trying your best. Do you realise how remarkable that makes you? People don't expect you to succeed and it's wonderful when you prove them wrong, because you will. Throughout history and in countless movies the underdog has always been seen as the least threatening person in the room but actually they are the person most likely to succeed. Embrace being the underdog, because you wouldn't be who you are without your story, your background, without all the obstacles you faced. Everyone loves a good breakout story. What's yours?

4

THE BIG BLOWOUT

Είναι φέτες.
She is "slices".

A blowout treatment is the creme de la creme of all hairdressing services. A luxurious hair service that transforms your dull locks from drab to fab. This is a special pampering hair experience beginning with a relaxing conditioning hair wash, finished off with a good old-fashioned professional blow dry, using a blasting hot hair dryer and a round bristle brush. At El Greco big blow outs always happened on a Friday night, when all the young women would come in to get their bling bling big money hair ahead of their big night out. I envied them so, sitting prettily up high in their skinny jeans in the swivel chairs, full of excitement and anticipation of the evening ahead, while Mama worked her magic. I always looked on thinking of my own evening ahead, wedged between my family on the brown sofa watching *Bullseye* and eating souvlaki, longingly aching for it to one day be me. And then suddenly it was.

A fresh blow dry or a good haircut can literally change your life. I mean it. When you know you look good, you feel good making you feel more prepared to face the world. My Mama had the gift of making others look and feel beautiful and she shared her superpower with me. She made me feel beautiful too. When everything else felt like it was going wrong, hair was my secret ammunition, it gave me something the other kids didn't have. It was transformative, life giving, a way to be cool. I think it's like that for a lot of people. Even to this day hair gives me a way to reclaim lost things and to hope for better things to come. There have been times when I have taken a hold of its strands and hung on tight for dear life. Life can be gruelling and it's hard to lift your head up sometimes, but I reckon it's a lot easier with a great shiny blow dry, don't you?

When puberty hit things began to really open up and change for me. The El Greco doors suddenly swung open wide onto a new dawn and I was transformed into an ass kicking Greek Cypriot Melanie Griffiths from Working Girl. My eyeshadow matched my belt, matched my shoes, matched my earrings, I started to take time and care over these pedantic little details that would somehow serve to elevate my social status with the other kids, and as for my shoulder pads, well you could see them from space. I was finally in business. I made my own money to buy whatever I wanted in, wait for it, Woolworths. I remember my first purchase, giddy with excitement, as I emerged with my very own bag of pick n mix and a Wham! – Young Guns LP.

I always made sure I looked good at all times. I fantasized that perhaps George Michael emancipated from my dreams at night might take the plunge and happen to pop into the salon one day. Just indulge me please. We would spot each other, he would look at me and I would look at him, there would be a sharp intake of breath, (probably from Sheila under the dryer choking on her digestive) and we would both just know… that his highlights needed doing.

My hair was backcombed so big it felt like it reached the stars. My Mama had cut it in layers that bounced and cascaded down my back every time it was blow dried. I was like a Greek Goddess on Mount Olympus. I presided over El Greco like a little cloud palace. No one could bully me here. At El Greco people saw me as important. Here I was needed. Here I was a somebody. I washed hair and I took out rollers. I brought ladies their coats and I made them signature 1980s Mellow Birds coffee. Olga with the magic hands. Magic hands, that's what they ACTUALLY used to say I had. That was a lot of pressure to have on your shoulders when you're just 14 years old, but I rose to the challenge of being a somebody. All my friends were at home on a Saturday watching *Going Live* and sticking up their Duran Duran posters. But not me. I was right here, revelling in my new found goddess glamour and grown up-ness.

At El Greco ANYONE could be beautiful. Even me. At El Greco for the price of a blockbuster video a girl could look like, as my Baba used to say, "fifty whole pounds". Like, even if you were like trog ugly, my Mama would "sort you out" so to speak. There were women who would come in looking like Demis Roussos that by the time they left you thought they were Pepsi and Shirley! My Mama was a magician, move over Paul Daniels. Whenever I was at the salon I caught that magic too. My Baba's words echoing in my ears "at El Greco you can be a bloody movie star!" I lived in hope.

None of the kids could get to me here. No one could bully me, or tease me or call me names. I was untouchable, shielded by a rotating orbit of perm rollers and hairpins, tea cups and shampoo bottles. I was like the chosen one. I got a fringe, and got to blow dry my hair, EVERY FRIDAY like the pretty girls. My Mama even pulled out a few T-section highlights for me in the front and even… wait for it… she bleached my moustache. Olga the unfortunate was replaced by Olga the fortunate. I was blessed and highly favoured. I finally had a stage where I could be the main star. Puberty, or "woman's experience" as my aunties called it, though it came early, had been kind to me. My little peach sized boobs finally got bigger and my meaty doner kebab thighs got slimmer. My period came at just 11 years old which propelled me steadily, but surely on the path to womanhood.

I remember the day I first saw the issue of blood in my white knickers, I was absolutely terrified. My Mama knew perfectly what to do; of course she proceeded to slap me round the face. Don't worry it's something us Greeks do. The screaming and the slapping, oh yeah, we're pretty casual about it to be fair. It's a standard Mediterranean involuntary act meant to have a calming effect on its recipient. My Mama slapped me hard, as according to old wives' tales it is meant to bring blood back to your face when you hit the so-called "woman's experience". The belief is that after "reddening" her daughter's cheeks, the mother blesses her with fertility while warning against extra marital sex. Since she has now reached sexual maturity by "becoming a woman," the thinking is that the slap teaches her that sexuality is sinful or immoral.

JUNE 1986

Dear Diary

Big news! Got my period! My mum slapped me round the face. She said she had to. My baby brother chewed my sanitary towel. It's ok, it wasn't a used one.

Also let me tell you about the no washing of the hair rule. As yet another cautionary old Greek wives' tale warned us as young girls, if water touches your hair during your period it could make you go blind. Learning this distressed me no end. I took great pains to avoid getting my hair wet during my period. I will never forget the trauma of showering and frantically calling my Mama up from the kitchen once when a tiny drizzle of water leaked onto my hair from the shower nozzle. I immediately thought I had gone blind scrambling round for a towel, terrified I had lost my sight. When I later asked my Mama how it was I still had my vision, in a very easy-going manner she replied, "Oh it's just silly old wives' tale Olga from the village". Great. I could have really done with this valuable information sooner.

Being a Greek girl was hard. The boys certainly didn't have to abide by as many dos and don'ts as the girls did. "Don't take Holy communion if you have your period as it's disrespectful" and certainly "Don't sit with your legs crossed in church as this is what prostitutes do!". I never recall my brother having to abide by any rules. He breezed through cross-legged without any tarnish to his name. He was simply told by my Baba to go and sow his quote-unquote (ew) "Wild Oats".

I always kept my nails glamorously long to scratch the customers' heads better during hair washing. 85-year-old Anne especially craved for me to scratch her head with my lovely long fingernails. "Ooh Olga give it a good scratch. That's it. I haven't washed my hair for a whole month knowing I was coming to see you. Oooh use those lovely long fingernails of yours." Unfortunately my Baba didn't like it. He thought my long talons would be far too enticing to boys. "Olga these nails are too much, sexy show off" he would say "But the customers like it Baba, when I wash the hair, it brings more money" I would say desperately hoping to preserve my beautiful nails. He was unswayed. I remember trying to hide them under my jumper from him but he would always notice and force my Mama to cut them with the nail clippers. Devastated and bereft, I would sob, feeling that the removal of my talons had ominously ushered in the removal of my new found pubescent super power. Much like Samson must have felt after having his locks lobbed off by Delilah.

I was a good little worker. I loved tidying the salon and making everything look nice. I loved my Mama lavishing praise on me when she would survey the finished clean and tidied shop. Mama and Baba taught us to be extra good to the 'big tippers'. Tips were everything to us back then. Tipping in the hairdressing industry is a common practice to show appreciation for your hairdresser's skills, time and effort. It is seen as a gesture of gratitude for the excellent service provided. I remember my pockets bulging with pound coins and fifty pence pieces from all the customers. It was the tips that kept us afloat. At times when we were struggling, it was the tips that helped us break even. I remember some days making up to 20 pounds in tips! That was a lot of money in the '80s. Back then many hairdressers like my Mama relied on tips to look after their families.

My Mama also taught me how to backcomb my hair up high, it always seemed to veer slightly off to the side like the leaning tower of Pisa. A bird's nest of a hairdo, inspired no less than by Alexis Colby in Dynasty. My swept up "updo" gave me the air of someone attending the Met Gala and not Broomfield school disco in Arnos Grove North London (the one off the North

Circular Road, you know near Charlie's old sweet shop and that chemist that sold random stuff like geranium lady talc that nobody ever bought). My fringe was painstakingly fingered and coiffed to the nth degree, so as to soften my round moon face and disguise my burgeoning monobrow. I watched my Mama and I gleaned all the hairdressing tricks of the trade. Soon, if all went well for me, my grand master plan would be that my parents would permit that monobrow to be banished too.

I really thought I was going places; well Woolworths mainly, when I was allowed to. I had it ALL going on from the Tammy Girl floral top to the hot pink elasticated Rara skirt from Wood Green market, right down to my red Freeman Hardy Willis red mock croc stilettos. I even owned, oh yes, the 1980s holy grail of makeup, the blessed Rimmel 'Heather Shimmer' lipstick. It was a sort of frosted coffee colour and didn't suit me in the slightest but I insisted on wearing it as everyone else was. I refused to be left behind. I was a feast for the eyes. If I had been a painting back then I would self-title it 'hot pink bird's nest surprise'! I slowly but surely found a new found confidence to rival that of Crocodile Dundee. On our holidays to Cyprus I ditched the dowdy me and strutted before our chorus of 21 cousins (yes you read that right) all mouths agape, in a red bikini bought from Tammy Girl (bearing the words "Hot Stuff" emblazoned across my chest). I genuinely thought I was cool, I thought I was tough, nay I was certain that I was Miami Vice material. Bizarrely I also wore my naff school plimsoles to finish off the look, but let's not mention that. I remember silently hoping that perhaps Don Johnson might spot me there on that Greek beach and ask me to become an extra in Miami Vice. Not an unreasonable expectation of someone such as myself who was indeed such "hot stuff". But alas, sadly it wasn't to be. Also my strict Yiayia was only 2 metres away munching a cucumber and on Greek girl purity watch. I'm sorry that now your brain will hurt and you will no longer be able to unsee this image. I was actually going places, finally my prospects were looking up and my (far stretch) Arnos Grove School fame rocketed. Unexpectedly and most fortuitously I also became the sixth form chairperson, this may have been/most probably was because no one else wanted to do it. I even started dancing at school discos with crowds of adoring classmates gathered around me. They were seriously impressed. I could tell from their envious stares that they ached to do the running man like I did. From big fat Greek duckling to lithe Gringlish swan. Olga was on her way. Finally I had arrived.

JUNE 1988

Dear Diary

I danced at the disco SO GOOD. I wore my purple tie dye t shirt and my leggings with flowers on them. Everyone said I was the best. I think I looked good. Maybe my life is going to be great from now on.

It's nice to look nice but let's be honest people only really care about one thing and that's the way you made them feel. They aren't that bothered by the way you look or your successes. People don't care about the expensive clothes you wear, how big the house is that you live in or the car you drive. All those things are immaterial. I've met famous people with everything, who were truly terrible people and people with very little who had the richest, kindest giving spirits I have ever met. So just be a nice human, nothing else matters. Choose to want to be known as someone who always lifted others and made them feel good about themselves. That act of kindness always comes back to you. "I've learned that people will forget what you said, people will forget what you did, but people will never forget how you made them feel." Maya Angelou

5

WIGS N THINGS

Αν η γιαγιά μου είχε αρχίδια, θα τη φώναζα παππού.
**If my grandmother had balls, I would call
her my grandfather.**

Ready for a bit of history? A wig is a head covering made from human or animal hair, or a synthetic imitation. The word is short for "periwig". The first documented use of hair wigs is around 3400 BC, in Ancient Egypt. Whilst body hair was a big no no, thick hair on the head was seen as a status symbol. Wigs were worn by both men and women who were higher up in society. This included politicians, pharaohs and queens. I have always been fascinated by wigs. Growing up surrounded by wigs in the salon I was intrigued by their transformative powers and at how they changed one's appearance instantly. I became obsessed with the metamorphic power of hair. I noticed how different hairstyles could really make you look and act differently. The wigs would all sit on faceless chipped black mannequins arranged in a row like guests at a party. Red short bobs, long blonde curls, a neat jet-black pixie cut. I loved trying them on in the mirror and then playing with my voice until I found the right one to suit the wig I was wearing. I listened carefully to all the myriad of voices in the salon and tried to impersonate each one perfectly. The various tones, accents and pitches all swirled together like innumerable pieces of music. I watched and copied the women in the salon and carefully observed their mannerisms. From Chinese Margaret's singing tones with her squawking parrot through to Toni with the short red hair, and anorak, who communicated solely through grunting, I was surrounded by vibrant characters out of whom came the most fascinating sounds. This spurred my imagination to play with hair and wigs and use them as springboards for creating different characters. Hair became a thrilling portal to pursuing and creating different personalities.

My Baba however was my greatest inspiration, as bald as a coot, but that Elvis Presley wig that he wore until the day he died empowered him, just like Samson's hair empowered him in The Bible. I always noticed how my Baba's confidence grew when he wore his wig. We rarely saw him without it, other than a quick glimpse of his shiny bald head as he went to the bathroom in the mornings or late at night when he removed it and perched it on his bed stand like a little bird when he went to sleep. Both men were my Baba, the confident and the not so confident, the one with hair and the one without. I understood hair could be armour and looked at my Baba tenderly, moved by the way he drew his self-assurance from his wig. I loved him both with and without it. I regret I never told him that. I wish I had let him know that he didn't need to wear it in order to be loved by me. I seem to have inherited this from my Baba too and every now and then I have to be careful not to hide behind all my wigs. I play less characters these days in my videos and appear online more just as myself because (shock revelation who knew?) people tell me I'm funny just as I am.

To date I have a collection of approximately 100 wigs. Some people collect miniature glass hedgehogs, some collect traffic cones, each to their own, I collect wigs. My most favourite one is a blonde balayage one that was given to me by a dear follower who passed it on after her cancer treatment. It's so glamorous and lifelike and makes me feel like a total rock star. Other people leave heirlooms and gold watches in their wills, aren't my boys insanely lucky that I'm going to leave behind a catalogue of motley wigs.

I have always wanted to be a character comedian. Always. It's the first thing I ever wanted to be. I grew up adoring the comedy impressionist Mike Yarwood who did so many clever funny impressions of most of the showbiz stars of the day. I would watch the great Victoria Wood, one of the greatest British comedians and all-round entertainers of her generation who wrote dramas, sketches and popular sitcoms. I adored her and wanted to be doing exactly what she was doing. I taught myself funny voices and accents. I played them all: Thatcher, Kylie, Cilla Black, all the stalwart '80s staples. I also made up zany characters out of my own imagination. Some of them were explorers on the moon, or archaeologists who scrambled around in secret caves, others lived glamorous lives as air hostesses. I would turn chairs upside down and arrange them to look like an aeroplane as I totted up and down in my Mamas heel's with my duty free goods, namely my Baba's half used bottle of Blue Stratos. I did mini shows for my friends in the playground and performed skits to Greek relatives, in ornate mock-Tudor sitting rooms across North London. They would clap and say "Bravo Olga". I remember thinking how much I liked the sound of applause.

My flight of fancy soared as a child. I loved dressing up in my Mama's dresses and jewellery and fur coats. I was always assuming different personas. I was always creating imaginary narratives using ornaments and objects around the house. My favourite was creating colourful sock puppets who spoke, unusually though I gave them very dull names like Kevin and Barry.

In retrospect the names didn't do the colourful creations justice, Ricardo and Alfonso would have been better suited. As I go through the hormonal yo-yo throes of menopause I ask myself, perhaps it isn't too late to play with sock puppets now.

Comedy was my thang and it brought me praise which I adored. So I taught myself to get really good at it. I'd write little plays and monologues and practice expressions in the mirror. At school, as long as I kept the kids in the playground laughing they wouldn't pick on me. It bought me time and relief from their taunts. My very first character was Margaret the mad garden lady aged five. Margaret was a vagabond who stored all her possessions in a wheelbarrow and made cocktails and magic potions out of grass. I still think of her fondly and sometimes debate bringing her out in the middle of Morrisons bakery aisle.

In 1988 the BBC were holding Young Talent auditions for "Going Live' with Philip Schofield. (Not going there, don't worry.) I was desperate to go. Baba sternly refused. We had missed the London auditions. The next round of auditions were in Birmingham and my Baba refused to travel all the way up there. He tried to console me, "Nice Greek girls become nice teachers, they don't parade the stage." He stipulated in his thick Greek accent, as he drew on his Rothmans "What would bearded Soulla who watches television with her 11 goats in Cyprus think?". Why Soulla watched telly with her goats I'll never know. The beard I understood. The trauma of missing out on that silly competition has driven me all my life. Don't mention the number of times ITVs *Britain's Got Talent* has head hunted me only for it to end in disappointment. "This is your year Olga" some green ITV researcher younger than a pair of my pants tells me over the phone. Still to this day. On my lowest of days when I worry that life might have passed me by, I can still feel like that 11-year-old girl who missed her opportunity. All I wanted to do was perform. In many ways working in the hairdressing salon satisfied that longing, being there was like putting on a performance of sorts. It quelled that yearning for a stage and an audience. I paraded around like a little lady with teas and magazines, I did skits and shows for the customers and they loved it. I mean who doesn't want a 13-year-old Joan Collins impersonator washing their hair for them?

There were so many eccentric characters that would come in and out of the salon, all feeding my imagination. There was a customer who would come to the salon called Bubbles. She was a tall, elegant lady from Trinidad with the thickest accent and most amazingly huge mop of black curly hair. Like a huge molehill. So big it would brush the top of the door frame whenever she visited the shop. She always wore a headscarf over it to protect it, but her hair was so enormous it barely reached under her chin to be able to tie the knot.

She was so mysterious and glamorous. I was never sure what her job was as she was never allowed to tell us, but it involved celebrities or espionage I think, or maybe I made that up. I can't remember. All I know is I was besotted by her. I made up a character called Alexia Stifado, a celebrity Greek rock star, a part time travel agent and fitness instructor who was loosely based on her. Bubbles gave me hope that there was a wonderful world waiting for me outside El Greco. Later the created Alexia would speak to me of a world that I had yet to see and taste. She spoke of her high flying travels across Edmonton Green, of Buck's fizz and of oh so glamorous Findus Crispy pancakes. There was more to life than just moussaka and taramasalata. "Olga" she would say in her broken English husky, throaty voice "there is such a place called 'Aberdeen Angus Steak House', it will blow your mind. One day Olga you will bring a special touch of magic to the world. You are gonna be a star, you gonna be a superstar. Olga, one day you will be me." Please note superstar was pronounced "stuperstar" because of her thick hellenic accent. My time was coming and it felt like she was passing me the baton. "Go into this new world. Go and tell your story!" She would huskily whisper to me in her shoulder padded white diamond encrusted suit. I also loved a dear customer called Dolly, a diminutive Italian lady who dressed like a Hollywood starlet till the day she died. You would never see her without a full face of makeup and her eyebrows drawn in. I still treasure the beautiful costume jewellery she left us when she died. I lived for all the personalities and theatrics the salon had to offer. I turned my brain into a dictaphone, I made myself commit everything to memory so I would never forget it.

Another customer was Vasso, a Greek lady with a deep booming voice and grey beard and a trolley full of bread and other random goods she had picked up from her travels. Some of the items looked dubious. She would always call my sister and I over to present us with some "goodies". We would always accept politely and then put them in the trash can soon after she left. There was rumour that some of the items she brought into the shop may or may not have been stolen. But nobody dared ask her that. Her voice and presence boomed through the whole shop when she entered. She also always wore her son's clothes. A hearty visceral character who always sat with her legs wide apart. Out of her, my mad, larger than life character Aunty Fanoulla was spawned.

My character Androulla is of course inspired by my Mama's first trainee assistant eponymous, gum chewing, dead-eyed but beautiful. I adored Androulla. She was someone I wanted to be like. God had blessed her, as such a double whammy procedure of a perm AND highlights would unfortunately have left anyone with dry burned out hair. But Androullas' locks laughed in the face of these engineered chemicals and stayed lustrous, defying the odds. Androulla was also deliciously orange from sunbeds and fake tan. I so wanted to lick her arm to see if it did, in fact, taste like oranges, but wondered whether this would perhaps be crossing the line. Sunbeds were life back then in the '80s. But I would never be allowed to go on one Mama said.

Another character Bambos, a primped up North London mummy's boy with goatee and football kit and lisp is based on all the many spoilt pubescent boys who would accompany their mothers to the salon. Now please bear in mind that some of these "boys" were as old as 42. Bambos still likes his mother to choose him pyjamas from Marks and Spencer which, unbeknown to her, he promptly returns in order to keep the cash.

Play has always been an important part of who I am. Play has always been a way for me to find a way from darkness to light. Playing has kept me youthful and joyful of heart. I hope I always remain childlike in the way I see the world. David Hockney said "People tend to forget that play is serious." Play is an important and healthy part of life. Keith Johnstone, the pioneer of contemporary improvisational theatre, tells us that the imagination of the child dies the moment we expect them to be an adult.

Play is important for children but it is just as important for adults too. It sharpens one's creativity and improves one's mood. Spending time doing things that bring you joy and pleasure has a relaxing effect that counteracts stress. Playing as an adult has significant benefits for both our mental and physical health. We often hear the phrase "Stop being so childish" but being childish often means to behave in ways that allow you to learn faster, be more creative. Childlikeness makes you more open minded to new adventures and opportunities, it sharpens your vision and allows you to have a wonderful sense of humour! Having a childlike attitude has actually helped me to creatively find solutions to difficult situations. In the most impossible of situations, play has led me to many EXIT signs. Having an ability to play makes you more flexible and resourceful when curveballs smack you in the head. And believe me they will.

Don't be afraid to be like a little child, incorporating childlike traits can help you to move forward out of a rut and unlock your dreams. There is an inherent joy in having the mindset of a child. As we grow older, the pool of our interest shrinks. It shrinks so much that we end up complaining that life is boring and that we feel empty inside. Nothing is interesting because nothing interests us anymore. We feel like we've seen it all. Isn't that just the saddest? Refuse to allow the world to force you to grow up and dull the most colourful parts of your imagination. Having a childlike attitude, we are naturally more imaginative, curious and able to play without a worry in our minds. Being a grown up is so overrated anyways. I still keep saying things like "When I grow up I will do this or that". I honestly have no intention whatsoever of growing up and neither should you.

6

HAIRSPRAY ANOINTING

Τα μάτια σου 14.
Your eyes 14.

Hairspray is the ultimate finishing touch. It helps the hair set beautifully. The epitome of the hairstyle. That propellant denatured alcohol hydrofluorocarbon shower of blessing that says "There you go babe you look like a million dollars, let me help you stay like that". The one thing we couldn't do without is hairspray. Hairspray is an essential tool for creating and perfecting that sculpted style. This wonder product has spanned the decades yet it still remains one of the most popular styling products around. In the 1980s hairspray's popularity rocketed with the rise of glam metal and big hair.

I'm not gonna lie there were some customers who loved being absolutely caked in the stuff. Some of them would even incredulously ask my Mama to even spray it onto their faces to help their makeup set. So much so, that my sister and I gagged from the fumes and genuinely feared for them lest they find themselves in the proximity of an open flame. That said, there was something so holy, so ritualistic, so ceremonious about the way my Mama showered her customers with it. The spray came down like falling stars, it was hypnotising to watch, truly.

Mama was like an angel bestowing all her customers with magnificent hairstyles. El Greco was not unlike a holy sacred space. I witnessed an intimate divine-like exchange between hairdresser and customer, the hairstyle and its creator, my Mama and the souls she counselled. She beatified and blessed all the customers, meeting their needs with her worn hands. She never wore gloves so her hands were always rough and brown from the hair dye. We always begged her to but she wouldn't ever listen. Her fingers were always big and swollen like sheftalia. I would rub them with cream for her at night. I remember there was this one customer with a rump steak-like face and two little drawn in eyebrows. She had at best a handful of hairs on her head. We would call her Lady Gold. My mum would spend HOURS doing her hair. She would do the back combing and suddenly her hair would get

45

bigger and bigger and there would be more of it, like a miracle. Like Jesus with the miracle of the bread and the fish. At the end Mama would get the Elnett hairspray down, she would hide it up top behind the plants because it was the best and would then proceed to spray it over her like holy smoke. The normal customers would get the cheap spray, but the special customers got the Elnett. The special customers? Well they were the ones who gave my Mama a little extra money when they paid. The ones who would give me and my sister a fiver here and there. Baba taught us to be extra good to them.

There is something so intimate and precious about surrendering yourself to a hairdresser's hands. It's a deep exchange of trust. The hairdresser trusts that you will pay at the end of the appointment and you trust them not to botch up your hair. But seriously hairdressers are a lot like therapists and confidantes. Hairdressers are the keepers of our souls' innermost secrets. They give us their undivided attention for an hour or two and make us feel important, listened to. Hairdressing is about so much more than what a hairdresser does with their scissors and comb. A poll in 2016 showed that hairdressers are the fifth most trusted profession in the UK. Everyone trusted Helen at El Greco. My Mama made people feel better. That was a fact I witnessed daily. It wasn't just about the way she did people's hair, it was more than that. It was about the way she made them feel heard, the way she made them feel loved.

Many of my Mama's dearest friends were her clients first. We referred to them as "aunties". That's how close they got to our family, that's how loved they were by us. So many of her customers travelled a long way just so that they could have their hair done by her, because they simply didn't trust anyone else to do as good a job as Helen did.

My Mama was and still is one of life's great givers. You will always find her making meals for someone who is sick or picking people up to drive them to their hospital appointments. She is the most selfless woman I know, sometimes to her detriment and we have to tell her to slow down. "Oh shut up" she retorts "I slow down when I'm dead." We joke that if someone needed a pair of knickers she would take them off and give them to them. I promised myself I would be like her one day. I promised myself I would make people feel the way she did. Apart from my knickers, I'm not sharing my elasticated granny pants with anybody.

Hair was my Mama's love language. There was never any precise measuring or pouring of lotions or hydrogen peroxide. Everything was guessed and estimated. My Mama did people's hair with feeling and intuition. She would spray hairspray until it "felt" enough until every droplet had coated every part of the customer's hair like an invisible blanket. "How much perm lotion

Mama?" I would ask. "Just keep putting the perm lotion till it goes curly." "How much hair dye do I apply to the customer?" "Use all the dye until the grey is gone". She dealt with customers' hair with such love and passion, like a cook in the kitchen who creates incredible dishes without weighing scales and measurements. "There you go love, you look bloody wonderful" she would say in the broken English she had picked up at the end of every appointment, like it was the ending of a prayer.

The outcome was always perfect and the customers were always delighted. Having a hairdresser as a mother was my superpower, I could always reinvent myself whenever I wanted. My hair was always beautifully brushed and plaited when I was young. Later as I moved through the precarious landscape of puberty and adolescence my Mama gave me the permission and freedom to experiment with colours and cuts. She would often tell me to leave my hair alone and that she wasn't touching it anymore, but I was persistent. I wanted brown hair with blonde highlights then auburn hair with reddish lowlights. I wanted a long layered cut and then I wanted a short blunt bob. I wanted it all. I was never satisfied and was always thinking of my next hairstyle. I think she knew that the excitement of reinventing myself gave me confidence and made me stand out, so she relented. I loved the thrill of going into school and showing off my new hairdo to all the other kids. They envied me and wished their mothers had been hairdressers too.

A new haircut brought forth the promise of transformation that would be seen by all. I wanted to be noticed by the kids at school, I wanted to have a chance at being beautiful too. I wanted to be one of the Claires. Every Friday I would beg my Mama to bring home some bleaching powder and hydrogen peroxide, which we always kept wrapped up in a plastic bag in the airing cupboard in the bathroom, tucked behind the boiler. It was our secret. Mixed together these ingredients became a powerful potent gloop, a magical sky blue elixir that we applied to our bodies to bleach out the unwanted ugly dark hairs. I would cover every inch of me. In my mind, the hair on my body was ugly. I wanted to be like the beautiful English nymphs at schools with smooth, milky, white, hair free skin. I would apply it to my chest and forehead trying to avoid my eyes and smooth the blue sludge onto my cheeks and sideburns and down onto my neck. I left it on long enough to bleach the dark into oblivion and leave me with the white, blond, barely there strands I ached for. Like a newborn piglet, or an albino, bleaching my body hair gave me a cathartic feeling. Sometimes I left it on for too long and my skin would start to burn. But I didn't mind. I taught myself to withstand the pain, because the pain meant the mixture was working.

My Mama helped to set me apart at a difficult time of my life with her skill and craft. I loved her deeply and adored her for it. Hair was my Mama's love language and now it had become mine.

We lived in hair, we spoke in hair; it was our way of life. Hair was everywhere. The tiny strands of hair cuttings would end up in our halloumi sandwiches and somehow accompany us home. I remember finding a bright red strand of Joan's brightly dyed red hair stuck inside my white Woolworths knickers once. Hair clothed us. Hair fed us. Hair became part of my nervous system, the ends of the hair follicles acting as receptors, passing outside messages directly to my brain. Hair sang both to my consciousness and subconsciousness. It both beguiled and permeated my innermost being. At night I would dream of multi-coloured coiling around me, gripping me, magically transposing me, lifting my body up and above the earth.

There are everyday blessings all around us. We'd appreciate the goodness and stability in our lives a little bit more if we made more effort to notice the good in our world. There are so many blessings we take for granted. There are so many non-material things in our lives that are rich in blessing. As human beings we have been blessed to be able to give and help others. We can do kind things for other people. This is truly a beautiful gift that always comes back to us in abundance. Think of the many close calls and moments where you have safely made it through a precarious situation. That was a blessing. We all need time to restore our body and mind, and having time to rest can be one of the most valuable gifts we can receive in this busy world. Think of the miracle of our human bodies, how they function, how they are made to heal. Every cut, scrape, and bruise heals in time. Make yourself still and focus on the magnificence of your body's natural healing ability. In life difficult circumstances always bring so many opportunities for personal development and maturity. Learning from our mistakes and growing from painful experiences is a part of the gift of life. True blessings are often the tiny things that go unnoticed, the things we take for granted and deem insignificant. The roof over our head, the touch of a loved one, the warmth of the sun on our face, a belly laugh. When we reach the pearly gates one day we will stop and look back to find that all those little things were actually the greatest miracles of all.

7

HAIR TODAY GONE TOMORROW

Κάτσε στα αυγά σου
Sit on your eggs.

What do you usually choose to have done at the hairdressers? Well, if you're like me the answer will almost certainly be "just a trim" every time. I've worn my hair in the same way for a few years now and it's pretty much the same request every time I go every eight weeks. You won't find me asking for a buzz cut or a red fire dyed mohawk. No. It's always the same as last time and the time before that. A good old fashioned no nonsense trim and as boring as it sounds I'm absolutely stoked with that. I'm no longer searching for that perfect new hairstyle to reinvent myself.

As a young child I was obsessed with my girl's world doll styling head. Oh, on a whim I would cut my dolls hair then seconds later turn the dial on her shoulder and more hair would grow out of the top of her head. I got bored easily and was always changing her hair. Now I'm content. My hair has stayed the same now for three years. Unchanged. Long, highlighted loose curls. Either I'm stuck in a hair rut or just maybe I'm finally happy with who I am and how I look. No more chasing another cutting edge style to bolster some new found thrilling persona I'm desperately hunkering after. No, I've finally come into my own hair. I'm finally at home with myself, sitting nicely, resting on my roots.

But what actually is hair? Have you ever given it much thought? Let me break it down for you. Hair is a unique and defining characteristic of mammals. Externally, hair is composed of thin, flexible tubes of dead, keratinized cells – otherwise known as the hair shaft. Internally, there are living hair follicles, which grow in dynamic cycles of varying length that are dependent on where the hair is on the body as well as on hormones and individual's age, nutritional status and environmental conditions. The main functions of hair is to protect the skin and the eyes and to provide temperature regulation. Hair also increases the skin's sensitivity to touch, including sexual stimulation. Steady on, there's hope for my rogue menopausal chest hairs yet.

Hair grows all over the body, except on our soles and palms of the hand; well unless you are my cousin Panny, in which case there is no surface area unclaimed by coarse, furry, Cypriot down. A balance of different kinds of melanin pigment determines whether someone has blonde, red, brown or black hair. As we grow older, we lose melanin pigment, meaning our hair turns grey or white, even balding occurs later in life. Hair is the only part of our body that is detachable, and unlike most other parts, almost magically, healthy hair regenerates, it always grows back when cut. Like my girl's world doll. Most significantly, hair shapes our identity. It is a biological, physiological and social marker of all the stages of our life.

It's also one of the first functions that break down when health declines. Cancer patients who undergo chemotherapy lose their hair quickly because the treatment targets growing cells. Hair is also one of the most common evidence types found in criminal investigations. I know this to be true because I found one of our dog's hairs in the family biscuit tin. Busted. Hair provides valuable information for forensic identification. In fact, toxicological hair analysis can also record evidence of how much you drink, whether you smoke or take drugs, and perhaps even how stressed you are. You should see my hair after a spat with one of the misbehaving self checkouts in Tescos. Beetlejuice instantly springs into mind.

Hair accompanies us through all the days of our lives from youthful, fresh young styles to wiry grey strands; it is a constant signifier of where we are in our lives. In fact I could tell you exactly how old I was and exactly what I was doing by any of the hairstyles I had at any one time. Bowl cut? Easy, age 5 starting school. Mullet? Aged 13 when I was going through my Glen Medeiros phase. Short backstreet boy haircut? No brainer, I was 16! Big perm? I think you'll find I was 18. Long hair down to my back? I was 25 and I wore it that way right through to my wedding day when I had a glorious updo. Short, blunt bob dyed black and dramatic fringe, that's the somewhat badly chosen and ever so brutal minimal fuss required hairstyle that got me through the difficulty of raising three small boys. Soft highlights and a natural wave? Oh you'll find that's me right here right now.

I've had some wonderfully good hair days over the years too, from the way I wore it long and thick aged 9 to the messy half up style I wore for a recent red carpet event. But funnily enough the way my hair falls now is probably my most favourite. It's hanging in a very natural loose way with some added sun-kissed highlights, an indication of where I am in my life. A good, healthy, grounded place. I feel like I've reconnected with the hair I had as a little girl and I've found wearing it this way is both hugely fulfilling and grounding.

Our hair is one of the first things people notice about us, it tells a lot. Currently, my scraggy pineapple messy bun is conveying a stressed out, menopausal woman writing a book she is petrified no one will want to read. You wouldn't want to see me right now. Trust.

Society's stereotypes tend to influence how certain cuts, colours, lengths, and textures are perceived. How we wear our hair is a very personal decision, but it's also totally public. This can be especially tragic if like me, your bleached hair once turned green on holiday in Majorca from the chlorine in the pool. True story. Hair frames your face and is one of the features that people notice in the first few milliseconds of meeting you. In a conversation, people's eyes are always directed toward the other person's face and hair. Happily, it's so easy to change your hairstyle so that it becomes a reflection of who you are and a sign of your identity. Your haircut, colour, and style all say a lot about your character and your innermost self. Hair is an expression of our identity. I can mark every season of my life by the way in which I wore my hair. I bet you could do the same. Hair is like a barometer, it tells you where you are at that moment of your life. Think about your own hair. Why do you wear it that way? How long have you worn it that way? Hair can be a security blanket for many people who choose to wear it long, or a statement if they prefer to keep it short. Hair really affects how one is perceived. Put your fingers through your hair right now. How does it feel? Is it rough and dry or does it feel silky and soft? Does it feel smooth and straight or curly and coarse? The act of physically touching another person's hair, or even your own, is a very intimate thing. Some people love it and others loathe it. It's a hugely personal thing. The only people to ever touch my hair are my husband, my hairdresser and my boys when they were very little. They used to love brushing their Mumma's hair. They literally fought over the hairbrush to do this. I've always loved having my hair brushed. It feels so soothing, it does the same thing as a scalp massage, stimulating the capillaries in your scalp and increasing circulation. It feels so good and can easily send me to sleep. I asked my boys if they might like to do this again for me the other day, but as they are teenagers now they were somewhat both equally horrified and disgusted at the mere suggestion.

Hair plays a key part in so many aspects of life, gender, age, community, social status, and occupation. Hair styles are used as a decorative function but also convey distinct meanings such as beliefs, nationality and politics. This fascinates me. But did you know studies show people with curly hair aren't generally taken as seriously as their straight-haired counterparts? Apparently straight hair is often thought of as more conservative and curly hair more fun-loving and relaxed. I have to be honest, I always feel more grown up and serious when I straighten my hair, I naturally do this for meetings. That said, I so love the way my loose curls bounce around on stage, rioting and rollicking along with my comedy material. Psychologists believe wearing your curls or natural hair says a lot about your personality; you're outspoken and someone who likes to challenge the norm. You stand by what you believe in and value your roots (every pun intended). They also suggest that people who frequently change their hair are often seen as adventurous and open to new experiences. A more adventurous, colourful hairstyle may signify a bolder, experimental personality. On the other hand, those who stick with a classic, low-maintenance style might be viewed as more practical and grounded. As I write these lines I am currently sporting the signature "nobody talk to me, my lank hangry mop head needs washing" hairstyle. Where would you place yourself?

Hair is self-expression and creativity, it's the ultimate confidence booster. Your hair enables you to communicate your true identity. Hair might be "just hair," but having the freedom to care for it and wear it how you want as an expression of your character can be totally life-changing. It gives you the power to honestly and authentically tell your story. Styling your hair allows you to take control of who you are, it's no one else's but yours. Practices like washing your hair daily, using styling tools, and treating your concerns with products to keep strands healthy, creates a sense of self-care and worth in yourself. Even for cancer sufferers who may lose hair due to treatment, the very act of shaving it off can give them a feeling of empowerment and taking back control. Many disabled people who may feel detached from their body often say they see styling their hair as a way of taking back control and feeling visible again.

Hair is an all powerful communicator. It tells a story, my story and yours. When I have felt especially low, I haven't wanted to wash, or let alone brush my hair. This is common for a lot of people struggling with anxiety or depression. Similar to going to the effort of feeding yourself a good meal full of nutrients. You ask yourself why you should bother? What's the point? I'll just eat whatever rubbish I can find. The same goes for caring for your hair. You may wonder why bother with my hair? But, even the simple act of washing your hair is self-nurturing and loving on yourself.

Having the sensation of water hitting your skin is life affirming. It can bring you out of your fog and make you connect with your surroundings and where you are at present. The pelting sensation of the droplets of water against your body remind you that you are alive. Washing and brushing one's hair during difficult times can be a profoundly comforting, healing and grounding experience. There is a deeper meaning to Hammerstein's "I'm Gonna Wash That Man Right Outta My Hair". This playful tune was inspired by Mary Martin's notion of actually shampooing her hair while singing a song – something she'd never seen anyone do. Eight times a week, before a paying audience, that's exactly what she did. An anthem of independence and empowerment. For me, that moment of standing under the shower, as the warm water droplets soothe my weary mind and scalp, eyes closed, not answering anyone, not looking at my phone, can be hugely meditative. I have also found it's a safe space to cry when I have needed to. Washing, styling, and colouring my hair is incredibly healing for me. It's a way of loving myself, of giving the gift of touch to myself. There are times when I have felt so low that playing with my hair is the only language I am able to speak. Just like how we use specific words or actions to show affection towards loved ones, so too our hair also has its own way of communicating its needs. Your hair love language is determined by your unique hair type and texture. Being gentle with my hair makes me be gentle with myself and vice versa. After nurturing myself through my hair, I feel re-energised and am able to see clearly again. In her book "If in Doubt, Wash Your Hair" Anya Hindmarch aptly says this:

"Taking the time to do your hair before a big day rather than picking up other people's crusty cereal bowls is one way of putting your own oxygen mask on first."

Disclaimer: It's important to take the time to wash and dry (and for the win) style your hair. But sometimes I'm lazy because, well, life. Sometimes, I go to bed with wet hair and I end up waking up looking like Hagrid in the morning. But to be fair, Hagrid's hair does have an incredible body to it, so it's not all bad.

Hair is such a personal individual experience. We all have different hair types, variations of a good hair day or a bad hair day, and the styles we prefer to keep. But one thing that remains for most of us is that we use our hair as a way to help us feel confident and powerful. Hair has a uniquely magical ability to unlock sides of yourself you didn't know existed, giving you more power, control and independence. Samson the legendary warrior in the Bible was renowned for the prodigious strength that he derived from his uncut hair. It's important to own and be proud of the hair you have. Find your self esteem in whatever your hair type is, whether curly or straight, long or short, thick or thin. It's beautifully yours and tells your story and your story alone. Own it. What you choose to do with your hair is your decision and your prerogative, it's both your strength and your superpower.

8

COLOUR

Ακόμα και οι θεοί αγαπούν τα αστεία.
Even the Gods love jokes.

From a young age I was always aware of other worldliness. Like there was infinitely more to my everyday mundane surroundings. That there was another sprawling dimension poised above me and my bowl of Coco Pops. I could feel it. I refused to believe that watching *Danger Mouse* and consuming Findus crispy pancakes was the extent of my existence. Though it wasn't a bad life I was just so inquisitive and hungry. Alongside my traditional Greek Orthodox upbringing was weaved in the exploration of handed down old wives' tales and omens. From birth I was acutely aware of the existence of a spiritual realm. Dreams carried profound meaning and were hugely powerful in my culture, a way in which messages could be transmitted from the Gods down to us mere mortals.

My Mama has always been a shrewd interpreter of dreams. I have always had colourful, vivid dreams and would run to her every morning eager to tell her mine. I'd love to see the expression on her face before the words would form on her lips indicating whether it was a good or bad dream. For example, believe it or not dreaming of excrement was always perceived to be a good thing. It meant something good was coming, a huge windfall or an unexpected blessing. Having dreams where you had died in your sleep were also an fortuitous omen. It meant a deep catharsis had taken place and the bad spirits who had been troubling us had taken flight, my Mama would tell me. I would always ask my Mama what my dreams meant, fascinated by the explanations that followed. Often she and I would both dream of those we had lost visiting us in the night. Later when we lost Baba so suddenly, Mama would dream of him too. I think her ache was so deep that she longed for sleep as it was the only place where she could find him. Sometimes I had childhood night terrors but I never shared those with anyone. Ugly creatures with wings and blacked out faces pursued me, their long spindly fingers pinning me down so I couldn't breathe. I tried to keep those terrible dreams locked inside me and willed myself to forget them, lest speaking them out loud would make them a reality.

I often struggled with sleep. I remember my paternal grandmother practising black magic rituals at the table to help me drift off at night. She tried many dark art practices to "fkalo don fon pou mesa sou," that is, to take the fear out of my little body. She would steep balls of cooking foil into a bowl of hot water and see how the pieces contorted in the steaming liquid. She would pull out miniature foil pieces claiming one to be an aeroplane and another a stranger. She both terrified and fascinated me. From the miniature silver foiled pieces she would be able to see the future or alert us to dangers in the present. She would also spit on us, believing it to chase away bad luck, misfortune and the devil. That's right, to 'protect' someone, Greeks spit on them. You will be relieved to know I've never tried this on anyone. Another common superstition was that a sneeze meant someone was talking about you. To find out who it was you needed to ask whoever you were with at the time for a three digit number. You add these digits together and the total number correlates to a letter of the alphabet which in turn gives you the first letter of that person's name. Crazy as it sounds I lapped all of these superstitions up believing them to be a gateway to something higher and bigger than me.

Growing up surrounded by my Greek Orthodox upbringing and the many old wives' superstitions and voodoo rituals, only fuelled my hunger to find out what or who was at the epicentre of this other life, this supernatural terrain. I knew there was another cosmos existing alongside my everyday experience of life; I just wanted to know who was at the heart of it. As a child, I had a traditional view of God. My perception of God wasn't about a relationship, but more of a distant reverence. God was more like an inaccessible revered patriarch, a removed elder I could never quite reach no matter how hard I tried. We had religious painted icons dotted all over the house, propped up on top of our television in the living room was The Holy Virgin Mary, benevolent in a cornflower blue dress, smiling down on us as we ate hot keftedes and watched *Knight Rider*. In the kitchen steadied by the bulky roll of kitchen foil on the shelf above the cooker, St Andreas, the first called disciple, with a staff in his hand, watched over as my Mama spooned ladles of chicken soup into our bowls after midnight mass. The saints were everywhere in our home, they were welcomed guests like framed pictures of relatives, protecting us and guarding us from all evil. Alongside the quotidian monotony of our everyday lives, existed a mystical universe where saints and spirits happily co-existed, hovering and presiding over us.

Throughout my childhood and oftentimes after a rough day at school I would run up to be alone in my bedroom. I would gather all the icons we had around the house, splay them across my flowery quilted bedspread and kneel down and ask God to reveal himself to me. I wasn't quite sure who or what God was. But

I was convinced that if there was a God then he could do anything, including visiting me in my school uniform one inauspicious wet Tuesday in 1991.

Truth be told I've known God all my life, a presence that has always undeniably been there. I've even seen Him with my own eyes several times. Once, admittedly, outside a kebab shop in Finsbury Park. A guy who was off his head with a cheap lager ordering a doner at 11pm on a Friday night, told everyone, including me, he was in fact the ephemeral ledge. Another time a tanned speedo wearing Jesus accosted me and asked me out on a hot sandy beach in Magaluf. Ironically, the said mortal tanned god even wrote "Jesus loves Olga" in the sand. We didn't date of course, as his chat up lines were too cringy, plus his trunks were obscenely tight. But genuinely, the very first time I had a profound encounter was at four years old, at the top of the stairs at our house on Holloway Road. I recall it vividly. God appeared to me in a very bright light, like a white floating cloud, and asked me to fly to him. I remember leaping off the top step and travelling up to him, my body an airy mass of floating feathers, defying gravity, it was like walking on the moon. I remember soaring up high to Him like a leaf swept up by the wind. I was caught and held fast. I remember feeling very warm and safe. Then all of a sudden, the light drew itself back, vanished and I was back at the top of the stairs again.

And then I saw Him again. That wet Tuesday in '91 at the age of 16 He came to me. Being severely bullied throughout school, I also went on to struggle with my mental health as a teenager. I longed for someone or something to come along and deliver me, to carry me away. I had bouts of deep depression and deep self-hatred. The loathing was so strong I would feel compelled to self harm. I kept this from everyone as I felt so ashamed, but it felt like the only relief I could find from the anguish that would torment my brain daily. I always had a niggling feeling deep down inside that there was more, that there was a God who would one day come to me. He would heal my wounds and calm my rage. I could sense Him in my dreams and in my waking moments and I longed for Him to make himself known to me. Like the unmasking in all the Scooby-Doo cartoons I had grown up with. I wanted to see His face. "Show yourself to me" I would cry out in silence, "I know you are here so step forward do something, you can't leave me like this". I felt like I was slipping. I had been struggling for so long and felt like I really didn't want to be here. I had such low self-esteem and felt permanently lost. I would pray and pray for my mind to stop whirring. I'm ashamed to say that the gnawing pain in my head would only subside with self-harm. It was a low, dark time and I hid it from my family. I remember being alone in my bedroom, and deciding I needed to know once and for all whether God was real. I faithfully laid out all my Greek

Orthodox icons on my bed and prayed the same prayer I had always prayed. "God, either you're real or you're not. If you're really the God of the universe then show me! Stop hiding and show me now!" I closed my eyes and waited.

I remember the moment it happened exactly, I was standing by the white gold leaf embossed wardrobes with the door slightly open and I looked up to the ceiling. I had this remarkable, wondrous sensation that it was raining, I could feel little droplets on my face, right there in my bedroom. I checked the room, the carpet, my bedding was all dry but I could still feel this warm rain on my face. I remember this moment exactly. It was undeniable. There was something in my bedroom, a divine presence swelled and expanded, filling the space. The air was charged with a thousand tiny volts. My hands felt warm and my fingers tingled. I took the deepest infill of breath, filling my lungs, my shoulders dropped and my mind was made still. I leant my head against the wardrobe door and remember a little laugh coming up and out from my belly escaping my throat and freeing itself into the air. My body felt so peaceful, my mind relieved, I felt I could sleep forever. Something had shifted in that room, from that moment the course of my life had been altered forever. Looking back I realise that God had met me and it was His gentle presence that had filled the room. I immediately called my best friend, whose father was a pastor. I went over to their house and together they led me in a prayer of commitment to Jesus. I transformed overnight – when I looked in the mirror even my appearance had changed, it was as if hundreds of little lights had been turned on inside me.

Following that momentous night, God began to visit me all the time. He wasn't a notion or an unreachable deity anymore but a person to me. A friend, a brother, a father. He gave me reassurances and revelations through dreams and scripture. I found I couldn't get enough of His word. I would hide my Bible under my bed and read it at every opportunity. Sometimes in the middle of the night. My new life in Christ flourished as I plugged into church and youth groups. I studied at *Kensington Temple School of Creative Ministry* and then joined the *Riding Lights Theatre Company* in Yorkshire as an actor. I'm so proud of my work with the *Riding Lights Theatre Company*, one of the UK's most productive and long-established independent theatre companies. Founded in York in 1977, the company continues to this day to take innovative, accessible theatre into all kinds of communities far and wide. As green, excited young actors we would travel in a large white van and perform in schools, theatres, hospitals, churches and prisons, bringing encouragement and hope through theatre. *Riding Lights* was the beginning of things for me. It cemented my love of performing and entertaining whilst uplifting others. I knew this was what I wanted to do for the rest of my life.

Having grown up Greek Orthodox, my family struggled to understand my new path. In their eyes I had been given a religion at birth and that was mine to keep and take to the grave. But for me it was a lot more than a new religion, my new found faith was a deep relationship with a person called Jesus. I don't think they understood why I was so invested, they didn't think it normal, healthy even, for a young girl to care so much about God. They loved me and were worried and afraid for me, I understand that now.

To my family's dismay, I didn't become a solicitor or a teacher after reading English at university. No. Instead I decided to follow God all the way out to serve him in the Middle East. I was working as a youth pastor for an Anglican Church in North Finchley before going on a short-term mission trip to Beirut in Lebanon in 2001. While there, I wept and wept, my heart was moved and I never wanted to leave. I fell in love with the people and the country and I felt God was asking me to stay. I cried continuously and uncontrollably and I knew God was asking me to serve Him out there on a long-term mission. Back in the UK, I still wrestled with the decision. I recall standing in my little living room dancing to the Clash 'Should I Stay or Should I Go' on my CD player. I remember going crazy jumping up and down using this song as a kind of prayer. I'm like "God now what? Are you seriously asking me to do this? Should I stay and carry on living a normal life here with my friends and family or should I up sticks and go to a land I don't know without knowing what I'm going to be doing or where I'm going to be staying!" By the end of the song I had an unexplained peace, I had to return. God was speaking to me in that still small voice He has always spoken to me in. I made the bold decision to move out there permanently, it wasn't easy and I was afraid. My friends and family had actually thought I'd lost the plot. I wondered this too, apart from that deep pull in my gut that assured me that yes, this was the path. So, I returned and worked as a missionary and teacher in schools and orphanages in Beirut. It was honestly the best thing I have ever done in my whole life. It wasn't easy moving to another country and making my life there as a young woman, but it was such deeply fulfilling work and I loved the people there with all my heart they became my people and my family too. While out there I met my husband, Paul, a fellow teacher. We became best friends and fell in love instantly. Together we spent a total of five years serving in Beirut in sport and drama ministry. We got engaged within three weeks of getting together and then married just three months later. Yes, yes I know that's quick but hold your horses I'll fill you in on all the juicy details in a later chapter I pinky promise.

When God opens up doors in my life, I just walk through them. People around me haven't always applauded or understood my choices, and I have found a way to be ok with that. Throughout my life God's voice has always been speaking to me, gently guiding me. I only ever really need His approval. If my heart is right with Him I know I'm good to go. I'm always sidestepping and hustling in a difficult industry but I'm ever trusting Him. We just figure it all out together as we go. I'm still saying things like "When I grow up". Maybe I don't ever want to grow up, being childlike has always kept my heart soft and made my heart open to unexpected opportunities. I think having a childlike faith has fed my creativity and given me a fresh perspective on humanity. The brand of comedy I create isn't unkind, it's observant, hopeful, it doesn't mock others, rather it's a warm, funny take on the relatable problems and personal eccentricities we all share. God didn't come to make me fully pious and Christian, he came to make me fully human. One of my favourite writers Francis A Schaeffer observes:

"The Christian is the one whose imagination should fly beyond the stars."

My faith in God is the reason I do everything that I do. Even in the most barren of times I feel held and sustained. I'm honoured to have used my experience as a bullied child to serve as an ambassador for the anti-bullying charity Kidscape. With this incredible charity I get to advocate for safe communities for all children going through bullying. I've always tried to show up as my authentic self, a woman secure in who she is and full of the love of Christ. I wouldn't ever force my faith on anyone. I'm just me. I love making little videos where I encourage people by making them laugh; I hope people find them gentle and honest. I hope that I can always share my faith in a warm, natural and real way. Never forced or affected. God gives me the best ideas for sketches and I always pray before all of my shows.

In my life the normal and the extraordinary have always walked together hand in hand. I genuinely feel like I have been guided through life. Even when things were at their darkest there has always been that promise of light in the distance ushering in hope, like the moment the sun is just beginning to rise at dawn.

I share my own personal story with people over and over, I'm not ashamed of it, I refuse to hide it. God rescued me and has been with me all the days of my life. When I talk about my faith people often ask how I'm so religious, I tell them for me it's not about religion but about a deep relationship I have with my Father in heaven. He is a friend I can call on day or night, always there, always listening. Being a christian has not meant that life has been perfect, far from it. There have been crippling moments that have made me want to abandon my faith and run for the hills. But trusting in God doesn't mean I'm free from difficulties, no. What it means is that I know He never leaves me. Ever. He gives me the grace and courage to handle discouragements. Bad things happen but He has never failed to turn everything together for good. There is heartache that I may not have understood at the time but later with gentleness and wisdom I see restoration and a pathway through the brokenness. God often gives me creative ideas through dreams – that's how I come up with all of my 'comedy' sketches. He is the funniest, the sharpest, with the most brilliant mind. Sometimes I run through ideas and things by Him. I'm no stranger to lack; there have been weeks and months when as a comedian and creator there just hasn't been enough paid work, but I still choose to show up and create work that will brighten up someone's day. He has always looked after my family even when I've wondered how I'm going to pay the grocery bill and feed my children. There have been times when unexpected envelopes of money have fallen through my letterbox or I've found tins of food I forgot I had in the back of the cupboard. He has always met me. I know I'm called to create comedy and bring joy and encouragement to others. This is a gift God has given me and I want to be faithful with it always. My life and all the things that have happened to me along the way have been nothing short of miraculous.

"There are only two ways to live your life. One is as though nothing is a miracle. The other is as though everything is a miracle."

Albert Einstein

"Miracles happen everyday." How many times have we uttered these words in our lives? We say it to ourselves and to our family and friends, but how many of us actually believe it? Amazing things happen when you least expect them to. A miracle is something wonderful but inexplicable. Impossible things can flip to the possible, closed doors can suddenly fling open. It's an unfortunate fact that our brains are geared towards seeing the negative, but that doesn't negate the fact that the positive is still out there too. Pay attention to those little everyday miracles. The sun rises and sets everyday, small seeds grow into great trees, the breath in your lungs and the food on your table. Some miracles are sudden and some happen over years, like recovering from addiction or a breakdown or illness. I truly believe and know from experience that miracles happen every single day. We just have to have the faith, the eyes, and the heart to be able to see them. Look out for your little miracle today.

9

A MAN'S PERM

Έσκασε έξω σαν κλανιά.
He popped out like a fart.

A man's perm. Those words haunted me as a child. Wherever I went the cautionary tale of "A man's perm" rang in my ears! "Stay away from the man's perm Olga!" I didn't know why I needed to live in such fear of a man with a tightly curled hairdo but there you go. Little did I know it was just my non-English speaking Yiayia trying to say "sperm". All my childhood I had nightmares imagining some guy with tight perm rollers in his hair and a pink hairdressing gown chasing me down the street.

Let me break this down for you. My Yiayia actually told me that if I sat on a toilet seat I would get pregnant. I believed this wholeheartedly, desperately trying to go for a wee at Bowes primary school, standing up high on my tippy toes to avoid any part of my little chubby legs touching the rim of the toilet seat. When I look back I think I was traumatised by this forewarning. I mean wouldn't you be?

My Yiayia was a stern rotund little lady always dressed in black, she warned me that the toilet seat was a hotbed of the male seed "If you sit on toilet seat, that's how you get a man's perm inside of you."

I blame my Yiayia's mispronunciation for my misinformed, slightly stunted and ever so delayed sex education. So behind was I, that I remember going to my local library aged 21 to read up on reproduction. Yes, yes I am that old that I remember using the local library.

Also reader that's right you guessed it, I was still a virgin at 21. Shocking much?

AUGUST 1987

Dear Diary

I have to tell you something. My mum got me A BRA.
It's shiny with a diamond in the middle. I'm so scared
that everyone's gonna know I got one on. It's the
hottest day of the year, but I'm wearing two jumpers so
I don't think anyone will be able to see it.

Well reader, not as shocking as the fact that actually I was a virgin until I was 28! I had a lot of work to do in that library. I remember trying to surreptitiously hunt for the information in the BIOLOGY section fearing the bespectacled librarian might either take me for an eager, budding scientist or a sex-obsessed hussy. I hoped it was the former.

The only books I found on the topic were the 'Joy of Sex' which to be honest looked like a nauseating soft lit 1970s bacchanal affair of hippy enjoyment and I wasn't here for that. No I was here for cold hard FACTS. Why? Because nobody had ever given them to this closeted, furry little Greek girl. There was no Google, no iPhone. I settled on a huge, sturdy, archaic looking book with scientific descriptions and detailed medical images of male and female body parts, surely this would give me all I needed to know. Ten minutes later and I dumped the book back on the shelf and left feeling overwhelmed and somewhat grossed out by the whole affair. I decided I would never ever do "it", the deed, have relations, get busy, to know someone in the Biblical sense, it was too much effort. From what I could see it looked to me like a lot of deep plumbing was involved and I probably wasn't the type of girl for that. I crossed my legs and made a promise to myself that I would remain a cross legged, loin-guarded, asexual, tabard wearing virgin forever.

I also apportion a lot of my late development to the painting Baba bought for us off his mate Irish Mick. This dodgy piece of "art" was hugely responsible for my opaque, skewed and grossly misinformed view on love. I now realise how terrible a work of art it was and I have no idea where Irish Mick got it. It was best not to ask where Irish Mick got anything, he was always turning up with random things in the back of his van. This painting was so bad maybe he might have even painted it himself. The painting depicted a lovestruck prince and a princess calling to each other across rolling hills, blooms dotting the lush green grass and an overhead piercing cerulean sky. I would fall asleep every night looking at that painting, wanting to be like the princess beckoning her prince from a safe distance so she could never EVER get impregnated. Phew no man's perm for her. It was most unfortunate that the prince was a tad boss-eyed as someone had painted his eyes a little too close together. Yes reader, this atrocious canvas was my very first introduction to love.

I was so very sheltered and so very naïve. It is no surprise then that I suddenly found myself "28 and no marry", as mother would say to me on our calls. Married and unmarried. This is the single most important human categorisation bracket that matters to us Greeks. Further to, we have the subcategories of children or no children, then moving up into the echelons of how many children and even (now we're talking) what percentage of those are boys. Being a Greek girl who was, as formerly mentioned, 28 no marry, was akin to having the black death. I would have taken the black death any day over the tuts and shakes of the aunties' heads whenever they saw me.

Oh of course there were suitors, but truly undesirable ones, a bit like our boss-eyed prince. The hair salon also conveniently doubled up as a dating agency as tiny Greek women with huge coiffed hairstyles were the mafia love bosses trying to hook cross legged, loin-guarded, asexual, tabard wearing virgins like myself up. There was Antonio the plain as mash, spoiled mummy's boy. His mother was always fixing his hair, acceptable I guess at like 5 but not 25. No, that creeped me out, that and the fact that her continual fuss over the contents of his lunchbox (all the double puns intended) verged on Oedipal. Our date felt like a long painful job interview. It was positively clinical. I would have preferred to have had every single one of my toenails removed one by one by a Barry Manilow impersonator than ever have to do that again. He categorically and ever so insipidly told me he wanted me to be a housewife who waited for him to come home from work everyday. True story. Suffice to say I 'didn't get the job'. He was one of the many promising (not really) doctor/accountant/solicitor offerings who were supposed to be every Greek girl's dream come true. Then there was Christos who I was set up with, he was by his own admission an "entrepreneur" who looked to me like he worked at a place called "dodgy towers", shifty and short with a monkey like gait, he told me he was just looking for someone to have hot passionate sex in the shower with. Lucky me. Sadly I declined. I'd have taken the boss-eyed-prince over any of them, any day.

Greek old women were always bringing photos of 'nice Greek boys' for my sister and I for marriage. Proxenia we called it or "arranged meeting". Proxenia is a very traditional matchmaking tradition that has been going on for many generations. Greeks are introduced to other suitable spouses for them to marry by their family. Once the couple agrees to like one another, they are engaged and then married. It was a tried and tested system, speedy and efficient, there was no room for messing around here. My parents got married this way, so naturally it should work for me too. Or maybe not. I remember one day a Greek aunt took out a carefully wrapped white handkerchief from her handbag and inside (I kid you not) was a photograph of a random Greek boy with a massive jaw and a hideous unibrow. The conversation with the mafia aunty went a little like this "Olga, listen, this is a very handsome and good nice accountant/doctor/solicitor for you ok? You very lucky to get this. Now just one little, little problem, oh it's nothing really… it's just his tongue gets swelling and hangs outside his mouth if he talking too much. But he is good boy, he from nice family." Deep, deep unspeakable joy. I mean genuinely, how do you even begin to respond to that?

I always prayed that one of the aunties would surprise me and whip out a photograph of dreamy Jason Donovan or Simon Le Bon? Now we would be talking and I would be open to offers! But alas it wasn't meant to be, the limp, wet offerings at the salon were always a lot more like Pantofli the 62-year-old wet, sycophant skinny, glasses-wearing accountant who always came and sat while his wife had her hair done. He would just sit and watch me like a drooling limpet as I helped my Mama in the salon. I wanted to make myself invisible as his pervy, beady eyes followed me all the way to the back of the shop. He would make me squirm as he looked me up and down, taking in my little growing boobs and emerging waist he would lick his lips and remark to my Mama that "Olga she make good development".

My Mama told us we needed to look good at all times as we never knew who was watching us as prospective wives for their sons. This was a lot of pressure, did this mean I needed to pluck my monobrow daily? I was perpetually teased and taunted by the row of beamingly smug cousins getting married in the photos stuck up with sellotape on the salon mirrors. Streams of photos showing well fed greasy cousins with too much eye makeup, swathed in white lace, like sausages in net curtains, would look down on me in pity that I hadn't reached their plateau of wedded bliss yet. "You poor spinster you" they snarled like snow beasts through mounds of hideous white lace. I was buoyed by the promise that one day, yes one day this too could be me too.

But a new chapter of romance unfolded and eventually 'black sheep Olga' ended her spinster no-sex-we're-not-British-but-nice-sheltered-greek-girls reign by bagging a handsome English boy called Paul. I had gone on a short-term mission trip to Beirut in Lebanon in 2001. While there, God was up to something, because that's exactly where I met my husband Paul. Paulie T as everyone called him was a cute tanned and athletic green eyed PE teacher.

I fancied him so badly I thought I would faint every time I saw him. He jokes that he took a bit longer to warm up to me. Funny guy. The connection was undeniable. We both loved God and we were both out in Lebanon to work with children and do good in the communities, we shared the same zany sense of humour and it turned out we were from the same part of London. He was, and still is, my soulmate. We dated for just three weeks and then got engaged. That was it. Three months later we were married! It was like something out of Hollywood Reporter minus the breast implants and dead first husband in the pool. But someone once said when you know, you know, right? Who did say that by the way? Smart cookie. But asking for a friend, how do you know when to stop boiling carrots? I had always said to God, 'Look I need you to find my husband okay! I'm hopeless, I can't do it, so please do me a favour and just bring him to me'. He did not disappoint. He brought the handsome, athletic, empty marmite jar collecting, brilliantly funny Paul into my life. My stomach leapt. I couldn't believe he was for me. Can you imagine if it was left to me and my medical library book on male and female body parts?

My family, suffice to say, were absolutely delighted. Despite Paul not being Greek they allowed the "Xeno" (foreigner) to join our family as, praise God, (A) I would be a spinster no more. And (B) wasn't necessary as did you not just read A??? I think they were just delighted that ANYONE would want to take me off their hands. My wedding happened the same year as the drop of the movie "My Big Fat Greek Wedding" where the main character marries a Xeno too.

My family took it as a good sign that all would be well and Paul's family all made sure they watched the movie as homework to prepare them for meeting my Greek family. I didn't have the heart to tell them that mine was actually much bigger and louder than anything they were watching on screen.

I always get asked why I call myself the Big Fat Greek Mother. Well, it's all because of my wedding day really. That and the fast speeding truck bearing three boys that knocked me sideways and made me a mother. I think I had no choice but to call myself the comedy alias Big Fat Greek Mother. It was a no brainer really. Call it serendipity. I don't know, it just seemed to fit. It's funny though as when people meet me they are always surprised at how small I am and expect my name to indicate some larger than life Hulk like stature. "Nah I'm diddy but deadly" I tell everyone. The Fat part of the name is always more street vibe in my head "Phat you get me?" Admittedly, I'm always way cooler in my delirious middle aged head, I'm way more everything there. It's a nice place to live.

Back to my story. So in the film *My Big Fat Greek Wedding*, Toula Portokalos is a dowdy thirty-something quietly wasting away as a waitress in her father's

Greek restaurant in Chicago. Toula has thus far failed to fulfil the cultural mandates of marrying a Greek boy, breeding Greek babies and feeding everyone; she has her family worried that she'll wind up a lonely old maid. Yes reader, THIS was me too. Everyone thought I would end up a dried up lonely old maid with double chins and stubble wasting away taking out old ladies' hair rollers in my Mama's hairdressing salon. In the film Toula falls for Ian Miller, a handsome, non-Greek, vegetarian high-school teacher. I fell for Paul, a handsome, non-Greek, all-meat eating, P.E teacher. I thank God for the 'meat eating' part of his personality, it was a huge sway in my family's acceptance of him. I remember him sitting and eating chicken legs with my Baba on their tense first meeting and I knew it was a given. My Baba scrupulously looked up at him from the oily dripping chicken carcass he was munching, to see Paul equally enjoying the meaty experience and nodded to himself as if to say "YES THIS IS THE ONE". The relief from my family that I was finally getting married, to anyone at all, overcame any anxieties they had that I was marrying an English boy.

Finally the zany, dreaming, wayward Olga was settling down. Finally, I was doing something 'normal' in their eyes and in the eyes of the Greek community. Thank goodness I wouldn't be a Greek lonely old maid. Paul was welcomed with open arms, as not only did he eat ALL the animals represented at Old MacDonalds farm but his loins produced ALL the sons, thus in my family's eyes making him a legitimate, actual Greek God.

My wedding day was a big loud meaty affair. The preparation was immense. I had taken it upon myself to fake tan my entire body to the nth degree; so much so that on the day of the wedding my poor sister needed to scrub me down with a loofah to remove the offending orange excess. I looked not unlike an Oompa Loompa. My wedding day was a massive deal to me and an even bigger, more humongous deal to my family. It was a proud moment. In many cultures, weddings are the most important event in people's lives. Greek Cypriots use weddings as a means of expressing their identity and connecting themselves to their roots (there they are again). It's a way of preserving their musical tradition and customs, history and beliefs. Weddings are especially important because of threats to my people's identity posed by Cyprus' long history of foreign rule and colonisation. Simply put, Greek weddings are massive affairs.

I had the very emotional Cypriot "Stolisma" too. It's a beautiful tradition that's been done at Greek weddings for centuries. When the bride is finally ready, a violin player plays a song that calls all the bride's relatives to give her their blessing. During this ritual, a red scarf is passed around the bride's waist which symbolises fertility. It's a moment of letting go of the daughter by the family. It was a very tender moment with lots of tears as my Baba was so proud to be giving his daughter away. He wasn't a man who expressed his emotions easily but the tears of joy in his eyes undid me that day. My Baba and I had always clashed growing up, he could unravel me like no one else, but I adored him. He told me and everyone in that room that he loved me in his speech on my wedding day. They were the words I had longed to hear from his lips all my life and he gave them to me on the happiest day of my life. Timely, considered, measured, but full of tenderness. Little did I know that less than a year later, he would be gone and that those inestimable, moving, precious words would stay with me forever.

I was overcome with such excitement to be marrying Paul, the love of my life, and to be beginning our lives together, yet overcome with sadness to be breaking away from my own childhood family unit. My Baba gave us an incredible wedding and I think this must be down to the fact that he had created a document wallet using one of my old GCSE folders with the words OLGA AND PAUL WEDDING written on it in biro. It became a massive project for him. His love and attention to detail was both conducive to pulling out one's hair but also massively endearing.

He even enlisted the top video guy in North London at the time, my Baba had only gone and secured the very best North London had to offer, oh yes: Video Tony. "Olga" he would tell me, "This bloke isn't just Tony he's VIDEO TONY." Video Tony immortalised forever, was responsible for spawning the most eye-watering 2003 sepia-touched-avec-elevator-music video known to man. So bad, it was good. Every time I put it on, my boys leave the room. They say it's because they can't face it. I like to think it's because they are overcome with emotion at seeing their parents being so relentlessly romantic with one another. Much in the same way they react every time I threaten to tell them about the day each one of them was born. Maybe I'll save that for their own wedding days.

I think we had the whole Greek contingent of North London in our house. All my aunties and uncles arrived from Cyprus with their kids. There were heaving platters of oily Mediterranean food everywhere. Rows of delicious pastries of spanakopita and bourekia to feed the hungry relatives. So much noise and warmth, love and chaos. My dress was so big you could see it from space, an explosion of white dotted with tiny, shiny crystals. I remember we got it cheap at a little Greek factory outlet at the time, off the North Circular road. A dark, backend place. There were seamstresses there with fags hanging out their mouths and Greek music blaring. I saw the dress and fell in love with it instantly, white, huge and fluffy like a massive floating cloud. My Mama saw my face and knew it too, instantly producing a wad of notes out of her little beaten leather purse and buying it for me immediately. It was the first dress I saw and the only dress I wanted. I'm impulsive like that, I've never regretted any decision I've "impulsively" made, with the exception of a hot pink sparkly body con mini dress, Magaluf 1998.

When we finally managed to get the dress home it seemed to have expanded even more in transit, like that stuff you squeeze into walls. It was huge. Delighted to have been liberated from the little factory, it seemed to spread its taffeta wings and take flight all over my parents' flowery three-piece suite. There was nowhere to hang this dress as it was so heavy, the skirt was so huge and the train was so long that my Baba drilled a massive nail into the wall from the ceiling, so the gown had the freedom to hang down and relinquish its creases. I don't know why I chose such a big dress. When I look back I wonder if perhaps I should have gone for something a little more streamlined for my tiny 5ft frame. But hey, in 2003 more was more. This huge beluga whale of a dress even had an unbelievable matching diamond encrusted bolero jacket with stick up collars which easily could have warranted its own instagram account today. As many brides with big dress fiascos discover, it was impossible to get to the toilet in it, my Mama helped me wee in a bucket every time I needed to go. Celebrity A-listers watch and learn. All that mattered is that I felt beautiful at the time and Paul was besotted. We both cried when we saw each other at opposite ends of the aisle, we just couldn't believe that we were one another's.

The day went by so fast in a happy whizzy blur, partly because I was so nervous and overcome and partly because my Mama had helped to heavily sedate me with Cyprus brandy. Despite being an English Greek couple we were more heavy on the Greek traditions. My husband's family didn't have a say and were swept up in the mad loud chaos, which I think secretly they enjoyed. We even had the traditional 'Money Dance' where guests would shower the couple with money in a wish for great prosperity. This tradition is called the "Kalamatianos". People wait to see whether the bride's family starts it off, then close relatives, then friends. Sometimes they pin notes together and pin one end to the bride and the other to the groom. Other times they put the money and a card in an envelope and pin that to the bride's dress. Man oh man what I wouldn't give for literally anyone to pin some money on this exhausted middle aged woman in her faded tracksuit right now.

We were so blessed we had enough to put down a deposit for a house. I loved my wedding. I wish I could do it all again. I often propose to Paul the idea of a wedding vow renewal in our back garden with explosions of white taffeta everywhere as our black labrador and nominated (by me) ring bearer precedes us down the aisle. I in a white tulle mermaid gown, Paul in a (selected by me) three-piece jacquard suit as violins and small Eastern European agile acrobats entertain our guests. Unsurprisingly Paul says it's a firm NO.

So just like Toula in the film I got my 'xeno', my foreigner and my own Big Fat Greek Wedding, and I have never looked back. I remember our wedding day felt like a massive explosion of family and love and happiness. I always say that the way my wedding made me feel all those years ago, is the way I want people to feel when they watch my comedy online or see me perform. I want everyone to feel warm and loved and welcome, like they've all been invited to one big fat Greek happy party.

After 22 years of marriage, the boy and the girl who first fell in love all those years ago are really still the same inside. Turns out, I think we did an even better job than the aunties arranging Proxenia! So much has happened to us over our time together, there has been sickness, crippling debt, arguments, silence, broken boilers, three boys, four homes, car accidents, poorly children, boredom, lost keys, bereavements, unemployment, anger, sleeplessness, bills, depression, broken washing machines, doubt, fear, empty fridges, panic attacks, cancer scares, nothingness, disappointments, floods, deaths, leaking roofs, hunger, pain, fear and worry. BUT through it all there has been faith, hope and love. So you see that boy and girl right there who fell for each other; well yes they are older, greyer and perhaps a little rounder and so much more weathered and tired looking these days; but really, truly deep down they haven't changed at all. Well, aside from my over plucked eyebrows circa 2003 growing back, and for that I truly thank God, nobody wants to go through life looking permanently "surprised".

But seriously there is no such thing as a perfect relationship or marriage. Please know that ours hasn't been by a long shot, but we refuse to ever give up on each other and find new ways to fall in love with each other every single day. True love has been my anchor and it has always sustained me through the storms of life. True love when you find it is unconditional, without terms or demands. To love someone without asking for anything in return. Ultimately, unconditional love isn't something that comes and goes. It isn't just a feeling, either. Unconditional love is a choice and a commitment that you make. There will be days when you wake up and you may not feel especially warm and mushy feelings for your person. Especially when they choose to eat a bag of monster munch next to you or offer continual helpful suggestions about how to flatten the recycling or load the dishwasher. But when you choose to love them unreservedly, you're willing to work past the absence of the feeling that you have at that moment and continue to show them love regardless. The greatest gift in life is to love and to be loved. There are many treasures in life, but honestly, I think this is just the greatest.

We all have our own paths and timelines to live through. Often this may not match the expectations of others. But it is your story and your story alone to live. I nervously took my own narrow path with much trepidation but it brought me out to the most beautiful expanse of happiness. If I had not taken my path I wouldn't have met my husband and had my three beautiful boys. When we scrabble around constantly trying to please others and be who they want us to be we never really give ourselves a chance. Fear of other people's opinions can make you play it safe and hold you back from achieving your full potential. Break the cycle and build up a sense of pride in yourself and your own journey. Cultivate a deeper sense of who you are and be proud of your personal dreams and aspirations. Oh and if you make mistakes that's ok. Mistakes are part of life and mistakes make you human. Following your dreams can be tough, I know, but not following them can leave you regretting all the things you wanted to do but didn't. Go for it.

10
A BAD HAIR DAY

Ο πνιγμένος από τα μαλλιά του πιάνεται.
A drowning man takes hold of his own hair.

Nobody but nobody wants a bad hair day right? A bad hair day is a day where not only does your hair resemble that of an Afghan Hound, but also it's a day on which absolutely everything that could go wrong does. You just don't feel yourself, it's as though someone has snuck up on you unsuspectedly and spritzed you and your entire day with eau de naff. Desirable thou feelest not. When your alarm clock rings on a bad hair day you would much prefer throwing it against the wall and scrabbling to hide back under the duvet.

Several years ago, Yale University decided to study the psychology of bad hair days – and found that our self-esteem was highly affected by them, with subjects reporting feeling less smart, less capable, more embarrassed and less sociable. I have had some awfully bad, nay let's call a spade a spade, monstrous hair days from the unruly misbehaving perm that should never should have seen the light of day, to the sticky up frizzy mullet that made me a doppelgänger for Billy Ray Cyrus. It was all acceptable in the eighties but never, ever again. I thank God there were no smartphones back then to capture the incriminating evidence. But anyways, let me tell you about a particularly bad hair day I had. It was so bad it lasted three whole years.

When I had my three sons everything stopped. After three traumatic births with each of my sons and the resurgence of past childhood trauma, my world spun off its axis. It was around the birth of my third son that the lights finally went off. I suffered a debilitating breakdown that changed me forever. I thought motherhood would be this idyllic scenario whereby I waved my husband off to work as I merrily sang and wafted about like Mary Poppins swathed in Cath Kidston, in the blissful domesticity of keeping my house beautiful, whilst finger painting with my angelic three sons. I quickly learned that motherhood wasn't that, no, not even a tiny bit. It was sheer and utter brutal, bloody carnage.

Three highly energetic boys in four years, I mean what sane person actually does that? I recall a blur of wandering around supermarkets, with three little boys hanging off me whilst I looked at buying pillows in the shape of succulents and random Pyrex dishes I didn't need, with money we didn't have to numb the boredom and sheer sleepless exhaustion.

The theatre stage became a distant memory for me, I was knee deep in lego and cabbage leaves stuffed into pregnancy bras, desperately trying to survive motherhood. My Baba had died during my first pregnancy and the grief had nowhere to go and put itself. It just hung around for years like an unwanted guest. I remember bleeding whilst five months pregnant on the day of my Baba's funeral and being told to stop crying by well meaning relatives as exposing my grief would cause me to have a miscarriage.

Unattended to, the suppressed ache, the loss, the layers of postnatal depression all rolled over into my second and third pregnancies. All my deliveries were long drawn out, complicated and traumatic. At 37 after an emergency caesarean with my third son, I started having unusual gnawing thoughts about my own death and mortality.

NOVEMBER 2011

It's gone dark again and I can't breathe. God, how many times have I asked you to help me? I feel like I'm drowning in deep waters and no one can pull me up. I don't even know who she is in the mirror. She looks like me but isn't me. Something has cracked inside. I heard it. I think it's me. I've splintered. I can't go on like this. I feel like I'm floating over my life and my boys. Boo, I'm a ghost.

FEBRUARY 2012

Please God make it stop. Why won't you make it stop? I'm so tired inside my head. The dread comes every day. I'm like a dead woman walking. There is nothing left. I look for myself but I've disappeared.

I can see now how I was hurtling fast towards a complete breakdown. I think I shut down in order to cope. My head was delirious and I was having relentless terrifying and intrusive thoughts. The more I tried to push the thoughts away the more convincingly they returned, unrelenting and ever more urgent. I felt like I was drowning inside my own head. Every time I tried to grab hold of an intrusive thought and pin it down another would attack me and bulldoze me down, I felt helpless. I started suffering panic attacks that would last for hours and sometimes days. My body would go numb, I would sweat and uncontrollably shake, unable to stop myself. I felt like a crazed insomniac. I remember crying and begging the doctor for sleeping tablets. I saw my nights out at the top of the stairs. There were two emotions I recall, dumb terror and uncontrollable pain. I can still feel the ache of that season every time I pass that top step.

To the world outside I was excelling. I was soaring and ticking every mum box there was. I was reading all the books creating all the right toddler recipes, and my house looked beautiful. I even made myself look beautiful, always doing my hair and make up. But inside, inside there was nothing. I would wearily push and push that massive double buggy, with a buggy board attached, as I pounded the pavements with my precious cargo of three sons. I wanted to do everything in my power to protect them from what I was going through. I didn't want them to know that mummy was feeling so sad inside. I prayed that they would be protected from the horror playing out inside my mind, projected onto a continual daily back screen of living terror. I didn't want even a hint of that darkness to come anywhere near my boys. So I jammed a lid down on it and bottled it up.

I lost the joy of everyday things, I couldn't eat, I lost so much weight I felt like a skeleton, shrinking into myself until I was nothing. I was convinced in my head that I was dying. I became obsessive about my health, checking and rechecking parts of my body. I hated undressing in case I suddenly spotted a part of my anatomy unbeknown to me that was secretly rotting, decaying, dying beneath the surface. I abhorred my flesh. I didn't want to even visit the optician or dentist for fear of them telling me that I had some hidden illness. I couldn't listen to the news or watch television in case there was mention of anyone ill or dying, as instantly I would start fantasising that whatever they were suffering was happening to me too.

The turning point for me was listening to my husband Paul with his head in his hands crying and saying that he couldn't carry me anymore. Everything had taken its toll on him. I had relied on him for so long to cover the cracks in our little family and carry me, to carry us all. In that instant when he looked at me I saw in his eyes that he had hit his wall. I knew then and there that I had to do something about how I was feeling. Firstly I had to admit to myself that I was unwell and that I needed to go to the doctor for help. It was both the most painful thing I've ever had to do and also the most liberating, admitting to myself that I was not ok. The need to be well exceeded the shame I felt to reveal to another soul the ugly contents of my head. I made an appointment at the doctor's and finally got the help I so badly needed. Life slowly began to change. Little by little the fog began to lift.

In that time the love of my husband, my family and friends, but above all my faith saved me. I would pray distraught prayers to God without my lips moving. I wrote so many furious tear stained letters to God in that time pouring out my anguish telling Him how I was feeling and begging Him to make it all stop and go away. Though He didn't make everything go away He never left me. I had to go through the most frightening, most harrowing time of my life, but He held my hand through it. His presence was undeniable. I kept hearing His voice telling me to hold on and to not let go every time I cried out to him that my head was going under.

I remember once travelling up an escalator on the underground, I was so weak and heartbroken I started to fall backwards but then someone caught me from behind. When I turned around nobody was there. I am sure that God had sent an angel to catch me. I still have moments in my life when I feel like my foot is slipping. There are times where I feel stuck and lost but it will never be like it was. When you've been in the darkest place nothing else can terrify you. My healing didn't happen in a matter of days. It took years but the work that happened within me was complete. Like the permanent healing of a deep angry wound. Whenever I struggle I go back and see how far I have come. I remember my scars. I know there is still so much road to travel but I have an empathy and love for others now unlike I ever had before. Many of us experience times like this in our lives, where we feel we are losing our footing, that we won't make it. Whatever you need, if you are feeling helpless, reach out, help is always available. For me, my faith and the love of my husband was what helped keep me alive and helped me to find my way back to where I needed to be. For others, it is professional guidance, talking therapies, their families or medicine. Everything has immense value.

The landscape of my life was altered forever in this long dark period and looking back I now know it had to be this way. Once I had completely broken down I could finally completely heal. There was no other way round or easy way out and I've had to make peace with that. This was the road, and this was the path to home. I just wanted to be honest with you and with myself about one of the darkest periods of my life. My very bad hair day, or rather should I say days. I want to deposit it all here. Lay it down. Lay it to rest. As I stand and look at this body of sadness, this expanse of recovery, I make peace with it. I go mouth to mouth and I kiss it goodbye. This is what happened and I want you to know I am ok. Maybe someone reading this will need to know that they will be ok too.

Accepting hard times can help you get over them. Coming out of your hiding place and admitting you need help is often the bravest and hardest step. Always remember that no matter what happens, you will survive and come through stronger on the other side. Be mindful and understanding of yourself and your emotions. Don't be in a rush to push away difficult feelings, sit with them and be patient enough to learn how to process them in a healthy way. We are often great at being kind to others, but what about being kind to ourselves and more compassionate of our own experiences. Also please know that you don't have to face hard things alone. Don't be afraid to ask for help and support from professionals or those around you. Don't be discouraged if it feels like things are taking a long time to get better. With patience and perseverance, you can make it through anything. This isn't forever. I promise. My Mama taught me that life changes every day. As difficult as situations can be, nothing stays the same forever. Darkness always gives way to the light and the night to morning. Hold on, tomorrow is always a new day.

11
HIGHLIGHTS

Γέλασα τόσο πολύ μου έπεσαν τα έντερα.
I laughed so much my intestines fell out.

Highlights are simply pieces of hair that are lighter than your natural colour. There are different types of highlighting techniques. Traditionally, foils are used to strategically isolate parts of the hair in various shapes and patterns, to create a contrast that's very bold, or very soft. There's also the newer more modern technique, balayage, where highlights are hand-painted onto smaller, more random pieces of hair, resulting in a more lived-in look. Highlights can instantly transform and brighten your style, adding dimension and movement to any base colour. In the 80s when I was growing up everyone wanted highlights and getting them was painful! Back then the method was those medieval rubber torture caps with a million tiny holes in them. My Mama would pull the tiny pieces of my hair through with a sharp metal needle. It felt like getting scalped. I blame a swoonsome George Michael and his tantalising honey highlighted do for making us all go and want one.

When I was 18 I attempted to do my own highlights at university and emerged looking like a cross between Bet Lynch and Simba from *The Lion King*. I emerged with my hair sort of all stripey, an orangey hot, fried, tangled mess as I didn't leave the bleach on for long enough. It was a truly horrendous botch job. The trouble is, I have pesky red undertones in my hair which always produce a ginger undesired highlight when the bleach hits. Now with time, many ginger fails and proper lessons from my Mama, I have learnt to give myself beautiful ashy toned highlights and I do all my friends too.

Highlighting my own hair is so important to me. People always ask me where I get my hair done and they are always surprised when I tell them I do it myself. Whenever I'm low or feeling a bit lost it's my safe place, my go to thing to do. I turn the world off, whack on a podcast, put on my old hair dyeing t-shirt and towel before getting my trusty Wella highlighting kit out. It was and always will be the stalwart that is 'Wella' for this hairdresser's daughter. Then I don the very same mediaeval hair lighting cap of my childhood and begin pulling out strands of hair with a sharp metal hook; just like I remember my Mama doing at the old hair salon. It's a long and painful process, especially the removal of the cap at the end, which disclaimer: may or may not rip most of your hair out, but it's oh so cathartic. In the end there is always the promise of fresh honey glow highlighted hair. Highlighting my hair always feels like a rebirth. Like a painter playing with paint colours on a landscape. Do I add more bleach or more toner? Do I need to knock it back a little with more brown dye? I always feel restored and renewed. By the time I'm done, I've figured out the solution to whatever problem was bothering me or received the answer to my prayer.

In life highlights are like your "best bits"; they refer to an outstanding part of an event or period of time. Maybe getting a promotion, or moving home, or passing your driving test finally on the fourth go. Ahem. I'm getting better at celebrating my highlights in life. The good things. I'm very much a glass half full kinda gal and have to watch myself so that I don't veer off to the dark side. There is so much to be thankful for and to celebrate. Not just the massive accolades but the little every day good things that feed your soul. Hot tea, my cosy bed, hugs from my husband and boys when they let me. Sunshine and walks, even though that sounds like something twee you might find printed on a cushion. Also cleaning out my underwear drawer is immensely satisfying; too much info? Maybe, but allow it. I feel we know each other by now. My midlife behind now has allergic reactions to any sort of undergarment that isn't brought from M&S and resembles something your Grandma would wear. Cheese graters, see ya laters! Also if I'm feeling particularly reckless I will clear out my tupperware drawer. Yeah I know how to live. These are my daily little precious highlights. Spoiler alert: these are the only highlights that really matter in life.

Around the time I was coming out of the heavy fog, one of my aunts was throwing out an old Casio keyboard that belonged to one of her sons who had outgrown it. You know one of those cheesy, clunky, clanky ones with horrific demos that should only be played in lifts in Las Vegas casinos and dodgy supermarkets in remote countries that you will NEVER EVER visit. I took it for the boys to play with, but they just ended up throwing footballs at it and head-butting each other with it. Little did I know that this little piece of kit would be my lifeline, my ticket to a whole new world. I'm not quite sure what possessed me but I decided to make it mine. Whenever I had a rare spare moment from the boys I would play with it and write little comedy ditties to the cheesy demos.

Then I started to create characters who would sing these crazy little songs, characters all inspired by my Mama's hairdressing salon. Then, I started filming these characters and their crazy lives and putting them up on Facebook and YouTube. People seemed to like them, or at least kindly pretended too, they were mostly my friends and family so had no choice really. Full disclosure, some of them were so acutely terrible I've had to delete all evidence of them; I've actually deep dived into the bowels of YouTube and Facebook and obliterated the lot. But... I can still deliver a belter of a rendition of my first hit (loose term) 'Shishkebaba Me' about a glamorous rock star posing as an inconspicuous dishwashing lady getting kidnapped by a handsomely dangerous, silk-shirt-wearing moustachioed mogul in a Greek Taverna; if you ask nicely that is.

With the birth of TikTok and Instagram my comedy evolved, as did I, and everything came together into a wonderful messy meaty little package. A bit like the Country Life margarine tubs my Mama forces leftover food into because tupperware goes against her frugal beliefs. Somehow, and I can't pinpoint the exact moment, but I went from Olga to becoming the Big Fat Greek Mother.

My Instagram account launched in 2016 and served as the shopfront for all the elements of my career. I never really planned to become a social media content creator. It wasn't my life's big dream, it just sort of happened really. As I began recovering from my breakdown, I started to think about how I could continue to show up as a comedian whilst being a stay-at-home mum to three little Zorbas.

I loved performing and making up characters that made people laugh, so I started making these quirky little videos – and people liked them. The opportunities began coming in, and it just grew from there. From performing at celebrities' houses to being on BBC3, on the radio and in theatre, I'm thankful for my rich and varied career so far. Things didn't really get going for me till later in life. My career only really began to form when I reached my 40s when I began to emerge from my breakdown, like a butterfly emerging from its chrysalis. I can't bear the whole "life begins at 40" thing as it's so cliche, but I have to admit that for me, truly, it actually really did.

I used to feel sad that opportunities hadn't come to me sooner in life. I sometimes wondered if I'd missed the boat but looking back I realised all things worked together for my good. The tangled parts, the broken parts, well they all sort of fused into one glorious, stupendously wonderful, magnificent, good hair day. Years later that metaphorical barnet of my life is still standing strong.

I'm trying to get better at celebrating and liking myself more these days. It's easy to jump about in wigs, and play characters as that's when I'm most brave: being someone else. People think I must be really confident when they look at my page, but actually I'm pretty self-effacing and shy about my true self. So, when I receive a compliment or praise or I am asked how I do my hair or about my clothes or my make up, I'm always taken aback. I still sometimes see myself as that ridiculed chubby monobrowed kid. Recently I had someone tell me they were in awe of who I was. I was mortified. I'm a lady who regularly plucks her chin hair and eats pistachios in bed and may or may not be developing a thing for David Dickinson on *Bargain Hunt*.

Because of my breakdown, I grieved because I thought this meant I had missed the boat. But now, I see my own beautiful path was only just ahead of me. A path I can encourage others to follow too. No matter how dark, no matter what people say about you, to never give up and always believe good things are coming. Because they ARE. I like to think of myself as a late bloomer, do you know what I mean? Wonderful opportunities are happening for me later in life now that my boys are growing up. I thank God my prayers were answered and they were unaffected by my breakdown, they have no recollection of their mother struggling. I enjoy them so much and we have so much fun together. I'm so proud of the young men I've raised and they tell me they are proud of me too. This has been the greatest highlight of all.

My husband and my boys are genuinely my biggest supporters. They've even been featured in my videos, for a price that is, these teens are smart. I remember once needing to do a stunt in a video by jumping over an ironing board. Naturally, I acquired the help of my middle, most athletic son to dress up as me and complete the feat. I was never going to chance it with my knees! My boys are always so happy to appear in my videos, in exchange for a substantial fee.

I'm finally at a place of safety, I'm not rushing or looking over my shoulder anymore. I'm embracing it all. I don't often mark my own successes. I'm brilliant at doing that for others, but not so much for myself. Now though, I see doors opening and me doing things I've been waiting for all my life. I have found joy and confidence again in the places I thought I had lost.

I felt like I had haemorrhaged so many years of my life due to poor mental health. For a long time I felt like I was always watching from the wings, while everyone else had their moment. Mine just never seemed to come and I felt forgotten. Maybe I told myself it's just too late for me. But those lost years are all being beautifully restored to me. Everyone's journey happens at a different pace and time. Can we normalise this please? We focus so much on time, because we see it passing us so quickly, not realising that we still have all the time in the world. If you want to go back to school, go; if you want to start another career path, do it. Don't use age as the easy way out. Age shouldn't stop you from pursuing a dream. It's never too late and you are never too old, no matter what they tell you.

"You are never too old to set a new goal or to dream a new dream."

CS Lewis

You might think it's over for you but what if I told you you were just beginning. Good things take time. Beauty comes from the ashes. Never ever, ever give up. I'm a late bloomer, yes, but I have learnt to embrace that and get others to do the same too. I don't want to be like anyone else or have what anyone else has. I want my own path and all the good things that are for me. Truthfully, things didn't really get going for me until I emerged from my breakdown. Be courageous, the best is yet to come. From great difficulty, beautiful things are birthed. Never forget the beauty in the ashes. Lockdown was a prime example of this. At a time when people couldn't mix with one another or go to places. Performers like myself were stuck in their homes. I saw this as a great opportunity to do Instagram comedy drop-ins for my followers. Ask yourself, how can obstacles be opportunities?

I would dress up and do weekly car discos in my car and give out sweets to the children in the neighbourhood. There is always an opportunity to see the good.

Be open and ready for life's surprises. New situations and paths may present themselves to you that you may immediately want to stick in the bin. Believe me I know! But don't be in a hurry to dismiss things. Sometimes wonderful things can come from those unexpected, insignificant things we either overlook or want to push away. I used to hate spontaneity. I like to pre-plan everything four years in advance; but that's a truly painstakingly dull way to live. Planning is important but so too is embracing the impromptu moments. By being outward looking and expectant, the most amazing avenues and doors have presented themselves to me. I've learnt to say yes a lot more to exciting ventures these days and then worked out later how I'm actually going to do them. We sometimes want to reject the future because it doesn't look like what we thought it was going to look like. But what if I told you that it was actually way better than you could have ever imagined?

Many of us find celebrating our highlights and achievements difficult – even uncomfortable. Whether it's down to self-doubt, fear of being in the spotlight, or not wanting to appear proud, it's common for us to shy away from recognising our own successes. We often don't. Tall poppy syndrome is based on the idea that, in our society, it's best not to stick out too much because, just like a poppy which gets cut down if it grows taller than the rest, successful people are more likely to be criticised. As a result, in the face of success, people can often feel inclined to stay silent to avoid criticism. Another restrictive tendency is imposter syndrome; the experience of believing that you're not as competent at something as you are – despite having success or achievements that prove otherwise. Feeling like an imposter or a fraud can make it difficult to celebrate achievements because you may constantly doubt or compare yourself. I'm asking you to stop and take a moment to celebrate all the great things that have happened to you in your life and all the wonderful people you have met. Gratitude is a superpower. Practising gratitude gives you a more positive outlook on life and it makes you happier and more mindful. When you accomplish something, no matter how small it is, choose to celebrate. Unconsciously, you're giving yourself a pat on the back for your small win which fuels your motivation and keeps you going on towards your bigger goals. Celebrating your small wins not only benefits you, but also inspires those around you. When others see you celebrating and embracing progress, they become motivated to do the same.

"The great victory, which appears so simple today, was the result of a series of small victories that went unnoticed."

Paulo Coelho

Don't be afraid to celebrate success, both your own and those around you. We all spend so much time being busy. We achieve a goal and immediately move onto the next. Celebrating success, however big or small, can feel hard sometimes but it is critical to going on and reaching even bigger goals and achievements. So go ahead and enjoy that highlight, you've earned it! Bloom big little flower.

12

THE VERY HAIRS ON YOUR HEAD

Πληρώνω τα μαλλιά της κεφαλής μου
I paid with the hair on my head.

How many times have women gone into a salon and shown their hairdresser a photo of a ridiculously gorgeous woman with fantastic hair and demanded to be made to look exactly like them. Also the women in these photos always have incredibly high cheekbones. This is sheer lunacy. How can you expect thick lustrous bouncy curls when your hair is thin and straight. Wanting to look like the girl in the magazine with a blunt fringe and sharp bob against her jawline just might not work for you and your rounded face (round-as-a-dinner-plate-face girl here speaking from experience). I often joke with my hairdresser every time I go in. I name a different Hollywood movie star I want to be made to look like. So, I'm five foot nothing and pear-shaped but hey I want a hairstyle that's going to make me look six foot tall and athletic please? Also don't forget I need my cheekbones to pop. Whenever you're ready.

There really is zero point trying to be anybody else but you. Appreciate who you are and value your own self-worth. My Mama always taught me to make the best of what I had, to look after my hair and always put my lipstick on lest I turn into a potato. However you feel, I promise you, you will never look like a potato. One of five sisters, Mama was content with how she looked and never compared herself. She has never been the kind of woman to ever push others out of the way to get herself noticed. In fact she often tells me her sisters were louder, more outgoing and more popular than she was growing up. Overshadowed in many ways, my Mama was happy to be in the background and out of the limelight, always content to be who she was. She always taught me to be content with my own beauty. She started working at 14 years old, her sisters went off to study but her father never had the money for her to go, yet she tells me she never felt jealous or bitter. She came from a large poor family and she was always content with what she had. I'm so grateful that she passed this grace and attitude of humility onto me.

Let me put it this way for you: a perm roller can never compare itself with a shampoo bottle, both do two but very separate and specific jobs in a salon. I've had people talk about having feelings of jealousy before but I genuinely have never experienced it. If I'm so fixated on wanting what someone else has, how will I ever discover what is meant for me? What a waste of time. Genuinely, feelings of jealousy seldom bring any fruit or reward. "Gosh, I just had an episode of jealousy and comparison today, wow, I feel fantastic" said no one ever. You and I can only control one life, our own. By constantly comparing ourselves to others, we waste precious energy focusing on others' lives rather than our own. Comparison really is that sneaky, good-for-nothing thief of joy; it leaves you feeling miserable and empty. Choosing to be ourselves fully takes immense courage, commitment and faith. Whenever I have chosen to be myself it has felt scary and counterintuitive and at times, lonely in fact. Choosing to not follow the crowd and refuse to mould ourselves to be like others takes huge bravery and determination. But perseverance brings great gain, because when we have the courage to just be who we are, without apology or pretence, so much of our suffering, stress and worry in life dissipates. There is no room for comparison because we are far too busy being our own unique, wonderful selves.

If I ever find myself wobbling with feelings of inadequacy I always seek out another person to build up. Similarly if I'm in a room where I don't know anyone and feel anxious, I always make sure to ask others questions and try to put them at ease. This always takes my mind off myself and helps to ground me. As I make others feel secure and welcomed I find they always reciprocate it. It's so tough dealing with feelings of comparison especially in the online world where everything is right in your face 24/7. If Judy went on holiday to the Bahamas with her hot boyfriend, with his waxed chest and overly groomed eyebrows then darn it I'm gonna know about it. To be fair if I was off to the Bahamas too with a hot boyfriend with his waxed chest and overly groomed eyebrows then I would also be posting about it too. But seriously, what about if I do see a social media post where someone is showing something I don't have but very much would like? Well, the truth is, I choose to be happy for them. I will comment positively on that person's post and as I do those feelings of inadequacy disappear. Try it. Celebrating someone is a wonderful antidote to jealousy!

I have always accepted who I was, even the times when I didn't like myself. I knew that if I was patient enough and kind enough to myself I would grow to love myself. I have genuinely never wanted to look or be like anyone else. I have only ever wanted to be the best version of myself. You can only ever be comfortable in your own skin when you make peace with yourself. I can cheer someone on who is something I am not and maybe I wasn't ever meant to be. It's about having forbearance and grace with, and for others. My Mama taught me that.

When you look at what someone has achieved in their life please bear in mind that you don't know the sacrifices it took for them to get where they are. We only ever really project our highlights onto the world and this is especially true online. We typically compare the worst of ourselves to the best we presume to know about others. I try to compare myself only to myself. I know that sounds bonkers but when I look back over my life I can feel proud to see how far I've come and how much I have achieved personally.

Turn off the unnecessary noise and choose to do things your own way. Back when I had my three boys there wasn't as strong a support network as you would find now. There was no "Instagram" or "instamum" phenomenon or anything at all to look at or measure myself against. As a first time mum, nineteen years ago when my eldest was born I was totally clueless! Well apart from a Gina Ford book I was gifted which made me feel even more clueless. My baby didn't want to sleep in darkness, he wanted light and action and noise, "Was he normal?" I unnecessarily panicked.

There weren't any apps I could go on or social media hangouts to check in as a new mum. Yes, I struggled, yes, I've spoken with you already about the breakdown I had when mine were little. But would I maybe have coped better if I had been on Instagram back then? The answer for me personally is no. I would have found myself lacking in every single way. We were struggling and in debt up to our eyeballs back then. I would have berated myself for not being like the other mothers and have beaten myself up for not having all the beautiful baby things I would see online.

It is easy to become so preoccupied with other people's images of parenting, decorating, cooking, or life in general, that you fail to create your own moments in real life. Life isn't about creating magnificently attractive and orderly memories, no it's about making dirty great big mess-ups. It's ok not to be ok, in parenting and in life. No one has it together no matter what they say, no matter what they post.

I imagine it can be overwhelmingly helpful sometimes online. Back then advice was scarce. There was no digital barometer for mumming. Maybe that was a blessing for me. Maybe now perhaps there are too many voices telling you what to do and not do. Such a cacophony of personal opinions. Of course there are amazing feeds and blogs out there who do incredible good; I have written for them too in the past. But will you permit me to say something as an older mama? I think it's ok to turn your phone off and just go ahead and make your mistakes sometimes. It's also ok to feel whatever YOU want to feel. You are going to make huge mess-ups, know that. Accept them and learn from them. I've really struggled as a parent, especially in those early days when my mental health was so very poor; it was a miracle how I looked after the three of them, but I regret nothing. This was my journey.

My boys are fine young men despite all my regrets and fears. Love covers all the cracks of motherhood. Somehow no matter how bad you think things are, you will all come through unscathed if you love one another and your intentions are good. Sometimes you need to give yourself a break. Turn off the noise and give yourself permission as a parent to get things wrong. This is healthy and normal.

So often, if we're honest, we all want to be known for something "remarkable" don't we? It's easy to look around us and see other people doing amazing things that can make us start doubting ourselves. But what if you could see all the wonderful things that you are my friend. Life moves a zillion miles an hour especially on social media, where everyone else's best bits go whizzing by. But what if you stopped, and saw how far you, yourself, have actually come in your own race, on your own little journey. Have a look over your shoulder. Go on. See, you're not where you were a year ago are you? Neither am I. Look at the road you travelled, look at how many brave steps you took. Look at what you overcame. YOU ARE bloody wonderful do you know that?

I know, it can feel intimidating when you look at your own life and it doesn't seem quite as shiny as other people's. But let me tell you, nobody's life is really that shiny either. Everyone is struggling. Struggle is normal, it's actually necessary and important. What if we started celebrating not just our highlights but our lowlights at the closing of each year? The things we wrestled with. The things that nearly broke us and had us doubled over, weeping on the floor? I think the pressure would come off and we would probably feel a lot lighter. We need to normalise lowlights and failure.

So there's room for all of us to do our thing. Girls, young women, older women. All of us. I was taken aback recently by two women who told me to my face that they categorically did not want to come to see one of my shows. They happily went on to tell me (in great detail) that they were friends with another well-known comedian, who they liked better than me, so they weren't interested in the slightest in what I was doing. I was slightly confused as to why it was so pressing for them to tell me this information. I wasn't unkind back. I just smiled, thanked them for their comments and walked away wondering how exhausting it must be to be those two women. It's so very sad when women put other women down. Just the other day another woman online told me to stop showing off to get attention. I'm like lady, that is literally my job. I'm a performer, if I didn't get the attention and engagement then I must be doing a pretty crap job, no?

Listen, I get it. Comedy is about personal taste. You don't have to like everyone and you aren't going to. But why do we still pit women, especially female comics, against each other? We don't do it to male comics half as much as we do women. There is room for everyone. I'd happily listen to the same joke over and over if it was re-told by different people. You see it's not the joke I love, it's the people telling it. They each tell it in their own distinctive way. Similarly I'd happily look at the same outfit on 20 different women. You see it's not necessarily the clothes I care about, but the person wearing them. They each wear it in a way that's unique to them and I find that so very fascinating.

So there's room for all of us to do our thing. Girls, young women, older women. All of us. I wish people would stop being so damn unkind and stop being so guarded through fear of jeopardising their own five minutes. It's so limiting and literally sucks all the joy out of the room. Stop being scared to big someone else up in case you get overlooked. Life doesn't work that way. I'm so very tired of it. Don't you know by now? Wonderful things happen when women genuinely support other women. That's how all of us get seen.

Some Greeks, especially in some of the older villages, believe that someone can catch the evil eye, or Matiasma, from someone else's jealous comment or envy. A person who has caught the evil eye usually feels bad physically and psychologically, they may fall ill. In this case, an expert in Xematiasma must tell a special prayer to release the person in pain from the bad effects of the evil eye. To avoid the Matiasma, those who believe in it wear a charm, a little blue bead with an eye painted on it. Blue is believed to be the colour that wards off the evil eye. I have never chosen to wear one of these because I can face this struggle on my own. I don't need to wear a talisman to make me feel at home with who I am. I'm already safe and protected and I don't need to fear other people's opinions. I know my identity. The Bible says not to cast your pearls before swine. That is to not offer valuable things to people who don't appreciate them. There are people in my past I have cut out who were jealous or manipulative. It took me a long time to wake up to this. Those people who were happy as long as I stayed small and quiet. But when I began to grow in confidence and see success in areas of my life they started to change their behaviour towards me. Sometimes people want you as long as you can be of use to them. As long as you fit in their box, well you can stay. It took me many years of being trodden on to realise that not everyone wanted the best for me. I refuse to be all things to all men. These days my circle is smaller and I'm so happy keeping it that way.

My Mama brought me up to not fear what others' portion was, compared to my own, to support others and never be unkind, to be content with what I had. My Mama taught me to hold my head high and never try to compete with anyone. She showed me how to be honest and to never put other women down to make myself look better. Of course, she put this into practice herself, by spending her days lifting the spirits and confidence of other women, within the little plastered walls of El Greco.

Sometimes we lose sight of what is actually important. We fight and jostle others out the way to be like the sun and to shine in all our own glory. The sun is bright, you see and easily seen by all in the day; we all want to be like that, to be "seen", to be "noticed". I've seen so many people get blinded in the pursuit of visibility. It's exhausting. But what if we try instead to be more like the moon? The moon in the sky is not obvious, it doesn't shine and attract like the midday sun. You could easily miss the moon in the inky black sky. Striving to be like the moon means you might not follow the crowd or be instantly "seen" or be "popular". But, being like the moon means you will be the kind of person who brightens up someone's darkest hour. The sun simply cannot do that. Dare to walk the path less obvious and make a difference in the darkness. Choose to be authentic over being popular. Stay true to who you are and you will light up the world, in your own way.

You are a remarkable being, individual and beautifully designed. You are the only one of your kind. An original, creative, imaginative being from head to toe. You could never be like that person you fixate on day and night, (aren't you tired?) and you were never meant to. Let me put it this way, the average human head has 100,000 hairs, yet no two human hairs are the same. Blondes have about 150,000 hairs. Redheads have around 90,000. If your hair is black or brown, you have about 110,000.

There are approximately 7,660,000,000 people on the planet but no two people are the same. Every single strand of hair and every single person is extraordinary and matchless. It's time to stop comparing because don't you know, she's just a perm roller love and you were a glorious shampoo bottle all along.

Indeed, the very hairs of your head are all numbered. Don't be afraid; you are worth more than many sparrows.

Luke 12:17 (NIV)

Mama
Baba
wedding
August 1974

Matchy
matchy
with my
baby sis
Holloway
Road 1980

I got it
from my
Mama.
Mama,
Maria and
I Limassol
1985

Mama At
The Sink.
Palmers
Green 1985

Perm anyone- El Greco 1987

Hot stuff on the beach. Paphos 1991

The lion king hair do
Broomfield school 1991

Scrub it
harder love. El
Greco 1993

This is
not Joan
Collins. York
University
1995

Riding lights
2000

My Big
Fat Greek
Wedding 30th
August 2003

Wedding up do 2003

Everybody loves
Helen. El Greco
2005

Hairspray
Anointing
at El Greco
2005

Not your regular mom
2012

We are open
El Greco 2015

El Greco
Of Hornsey
Edinburgh
Fringe 2021

On location Sunny
Bank Mills 2022

Big boy
Bambos live
at King's
Cross 2023

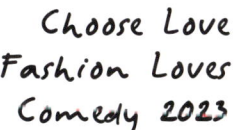

Choose Love
Fashion Loves
Comedy 2023

Everyones
Big Fat
Greek
Mother
2023

Androulla &
Chlamydia
take the
stage London
2024

Knicker
flinging with
Fanoulla
London show
2024

My Big
Fat Greek
Menopause
2024

Shiny lady 2024

El Greco The dynasty
of Hornsey 1989

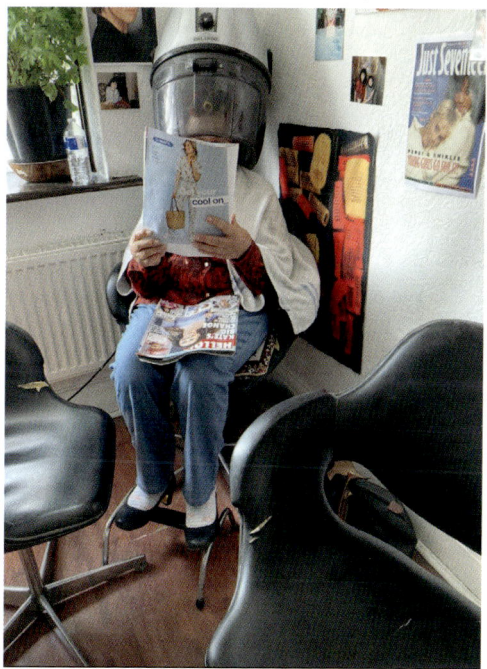

One lump
or two
El Greco
2021

SHISHKEBABA ME
2022

Take care of yourself but then always help others. Lift up, encourage and support other women. There is no budge on that; just do it. If you see another woman struggling to blow her own trumpet, maybe you could do it for her! Cultivate a spirit of generosity and encouragement of others. Give freely without worrying, it will always find its way back to you. When we compare ourselves to others, we focus on what we're not good at, rather than on our own strengths and giftings. Do everything in kindness and love. It's been proven that those of us who extend kindness and compassion have increased wellbeing and happiness. Kindness also helps reduce stress and improves our emotional wellbeing. There is room for everyone, so look out for others, you won't be overlooked. This is how we really flourish, not when we grow alone, but when we grow together.

13

SPLIT ENDS

Εφαγα πόρτα
I ate door.

Split ends are annoying aren't they? They get in the way of your intended luscious Rapunzel-like hair growth. They are just downright irritating. Split ends can happen to anyone at any time, they do not discriminate when it comes to race, age or gender. While hair is generally strong, it is still susceptible to damage from wear and tear, washing and sun damage. This damage, known as split ends, occurs at the end of your hair since that is where the oldest and most fragile strands of your hair reside. As a teenager I used to painstakingly snip my own split ends with tiny nail scissors, next to my Argos desk lamp, in a desperate bid to keep my hair as long as possible and avoid having my Mama cut it properly. Now I just go for regular trims every six to eight weeks like a normal person.

In an attempt to maintain beautiful-looking hair, people end up using products that claim to promote hair health, but unfortunately, may end up doing the opposite instead. Over styling and product overuse are also culprits. When damage occurs to your hair, it results in it becoming weak and prone to breakage or splitting. This can lead to unhealthy or frizzy-looking hair. Eventually, thinning of the hair and bald spots may occur as a result of the continuing and untreated damage. That's not good my friend. The only way to deal with split ends is by cutting the hair.

When applying this to our own lives it's clear that a sort of pruning back is required to remove the dry, dead things that no longer serve us and let me tell you it's painful. Bear with me, I'm afraid I'm not done with the hair metaphors and puns just yet but I promise to draw the line at "Hair we go", if you ever hear me use this then you have permission to cancel me and burn this book.

When I was going through my mental health battle, in the very eye of that storm where I felt like I had totally lost myself, I felt like I had literally split in two. I felt there was almost some sort of hairline crack running through my soul. I remember actually hearing that faint crack and crying out in pain. I felt like my insides were made up of lots of tiny sharp pieces. Getting up every day was a battle with a body that felt like a bag of broken glass.

When I went through that breakdown something happened to me and I was forever altered. I learnt how to become ok with not being ok. My experience had schooled me to see there is beauty in the broken things. Kintsugi is a Japanese art that repairs broken pottery with gold, rendering a new piece that is more exquisite than it was before the break. It literally means to join with gold. That's what I felt had actually happened to me at that time. I became stronger and more beautiful because of my scars, because of the cracks and tears. I don't think I would be the woman I am today had it not been for this shattering, this splitting deep within my being. I had hit the very bottom, there was no lower, my knees scraping the cold hard ground. But from there there was only up. Hitting rock bottom signified a point in my life where everything that could have happened to me did happen. I had genuinely reached the point where I could honestly say "It can't get any worse". The thing with reaching such a desperate place is that it gives you a new perspective on life, you're thankful to be alive and you can boldly say that you survived whatever it is that you went through. I began to reconnect with my Mama's childhood words of wisdom, the things she had taught me and that quirky little hairdressing salon, El Greco Of Hornsey. I began to make skits and write comedy and tell the story of my childhood and people listened and resonated.

Sometimes in those dark places, in those in between spaces where you feel lost, is often where the hope actually lies I think. It embeds itself right there in the overlooked spaces, in the crevices and cracks. Those unexpected pockets of gold embedded deep inside the fissures of your despair. Telling my story has always given people hope and it's given me a way of piecing myself back together again. Unravelling is healing. My experience, my faith, my mother's love, words and actions in that ramshackle little hair salon stayed with me and enabled me to mend all the split ends of my life.

Nothing we go through in life is ever wasted, even the messy broken parts. My Mama taught me that everything had value. Growing up on the farm in Cyprus, she was one of 10 children. My grandparents were very poor and had a lot of mouths to feed. Suffice to say there were no leftovers and nothing was wasted. Anything that remained – oil, animal bones, bread – was used by my Yiayia as the basis for the next day's supper. I even remember when she visited us years later in the UK with my Bapou, how she would hang all our used tea bags out on the washing line to dry to be used again, resulting in a very weak cup of tea my Baba point blank refused to drink. In today's fast society everything has such a short shelf-life; food, age, clothing, beauty, popularity, social media stardom. We have a tendency to throw so much away. This also extends to our life experiences too; we tend to want to bin the parts of our lives that aren't 'working' and tip away leftovers of situations that we haven't been patient enough to allow to run their full course.

My Mama taught me to be still and to wait things out. I saw her struggles and determination despite lack, heartache and loss. The way she would superhumanly make all the ends meet. There were days when the money just wasn't enough and the bills were many. She was clever and resourceful working on Sundays to do bridal hair and visiting old people's homes on Mondays to cut pensioners hair to top us up. She was frugal, making delicious food even when the ingredients were few. In my Mama's eyes there was no 'sell by date'. She saw and seized opportunities that others overlooked. She saw value in the discarded. She taught me that nothing is ever wasted. Everything we go through, if we allow it, becomes beautiful in its own time. All those leftovers of our lives were gathered up to make the most beautiful, hearty meal.

My Yiayia taught my Mama how to feast in barren times and she in turn taught this to me. Like my Yiayia I want to use up every last scrap of food, whereas before I was probably careless and wasteful. I have been thinking of my life in this way too. I once was someone who was quick to want to bin the parts of my life that weren't 'working' and tip away leftovers of situations that I haven't been patient enough to allow to run their full course. I once even felt like whacking a great big 'sell by date' on my dreams.

If you feel like me I want to encourage you to recognise that this is not the true picture for either of us. Nothing we go through is ever really wasted; even those very raw and confusing experiences. Even in difficult seasons all those leftovers of your life are being gathered up to make the most beautiful, hearty meal. All those bizarre, painful, mismatched ingredients of your experiences are not going to be wasted. Not a single crumb. Everything becomes more precious, richer, considered, slower. After living for years stuck with what I thought were leftovers, I saw my life for what it was, that I had been in fact richly feasting all along. I was left with no other option than to see the truth that was right under my nose. I do not have a 'sell by date'. I've stopped putting pressure on myself to do or be anything by a certain date. I've stopped grabbing each day by the neck, gripping it tightly and strangling it until it yielded me something. I've simply allowed life to breathe, I've allowed myself to take in air, to take the space and just be.

I was asked the other day where I find the confidence to do what I do. How is it that I can be so bold and fearless in all the videos I make? The truth is, yes I'm bold and yes, I'm always being funny today because I know what rock bottom feels like. Nothing can terrify me anymore. I always go back to my favourite Robin Williams quote:

"I think the saddest people always try their hardest to make people happy because they know what it's like to feel absolutely worthless and they don't want anyone else to feel like that."

Robin Williams

You see I know what pitch black looks like, I've been there and I've found the light. I never want anyone to feel the way I once did and if they do, well then I want them to know they aren't alone. I am known for being a Big Fat Greek Mother who makes people laugh. But I am also a woman who has had to overcome many mental health battles in her life. My courage, happy-go-lucky nature and a desire to make people laugh came out of one of the lowest points of my life. Tragedy and comedy are such bedfellows. This is why I do what I do.

I wanted to share my story with you to encourage you if you need it. Life as a late bloomer, for me, everything in my life has been very, very slow. Growth by nature is slow, it is never overnight, often it meanders, winds off, dips, ebbs and flows. I have felt overlooked and forgotten so many times in my life. So many 'almosts', so many 'nos' but I refuse to let the disappointment and hardships define me.

Life is unpredictable and those dry seasons will come. When they do, don't numb yourself to your own feelings. Talk about them. Write about them. Cry. Draw. Listen to music. Allow yourself to feel. Everyone who is going through tough times has a choice: What are you going to focus on? You can look at your situation as an end or as a beginning. You can see it as a curse or as a blessing. Every experience of your life has gifts for you. Take care of yourself and your loved ones especially during tough times. Mindfulness practices like prayer or meditation can clear your head and stabilise your mood. Exercise or even just taking a walk, can help release stress and increase your energy. The people you surround yourself with have a real impact on your mood and your mindset. Good friends who are there for you in tough times provide a shoulder to cry on and can help you to make sense of difficult times. Dry arid seasons aren't forever, change will come.

Trials perfect us. Difficulties show us what is most important in our lives. I cling onto my husband and boys more than ever. They are my treasure. Each crisis is an opportunity to practise more love, compassion and care. My recovery from the toughest times of my life has made me who I am. Life's knocks have taught me to respond to situations with humility and grace.

No matter what your story or your age is, or how many obstacles and drawbacks you have had along the way, lift your head and choose to persevere. You can do this. You can do the hard things. Split ends bring new beginnings. Look up and see what is waiting for you just ahead in the distance. It's yours.

"Try again. Fail again. Fail better."

Samuel Beckett

Consider for a moment that there is no such thing as failure. Success or failure is so binary, it's so black and white with no grey areas. Actually failure is something to be proud of. Failure can often lead to even greater success in your life. It all comes down to perspective and what you learn from your failure.

Failure shows you tried, it shows you cared and that you didn't give up. It is very much a part of the journey to success. Great things in life can take a while to get right.

Next time you fail, celebrate it because it means you're almost there.

14

YOU HAD ME AT THE FRINGE

Σου κάνει την ζωή πατίνι.
It makes your life a roller skate.

A fringe can change your look without cutting the rest of your hair. Fringes date back even to Ancient Egypt where monarchs and their Gods were already wearing fringe hairstyles, as depicted on many wall paintings at the pyramids. Farah Fawcett's fluffy 1970s *Charlie's Angel* fringe has inspired countless haircuts through the years. Audrey Tautou sported the coolest of bobs and ultra-cropped baby bangs while playing the titular character in Amélie, her chic French look became one of the most iconic in pop culture history. Of course I couldn't talk about fringes without mentioning Leonard Nimoy as Spock in *Star Trek*, his bangs were unbelievable and seemed to have acquired a cult status all of their own which has certainly lived long and prospered well throughout history.

A fringe, or bangs, can instantly transform your look and add personality to your hair. It can frame your face; a fringe can accentuate or hide certain facial features, such as your nose or eyes. For example, side-sweeping bangs can draw attention to your cheekbones and eyes. A fringe can also help camouflage a high forehead. A fringe can even make long, thin faces appear fuller. The right fringe for you all depends on your face shape, hair type, eyebrow position, eye shape, and overall hairstyle. From thick peekaboo bangs to long layered curtain bangs there is a fringe for everyone. If you want one that is.

When you watch my sketches online it can feel like they sort of just suddenly appear out of nowhere; well yes they do. There they pop on your feeds! A bit like in a hair salon, the colourist is out front performing their magic, soothing your week's woes away and carefully adding foil after foil to your hair whilst ensuring you are sat with a nice cup of coffee. Suddenly you see the incredible finished effect. Look out the back though and you will likely be greeted with an array of model mannequin heads with failed colour attempts, a pile of dirty colour bowls, half torn foils and coffee cups, all stacked in the sink. Well making comedy content is actually a lot like that. There is a lot of chaos and clutter in the background to making content. Often a 30 second reel can take a whole day to create. Contrary to your social media feeds, videos don't just appear out of nowhere.

I get ideas for sketches as I go, often at random times and in random places. On the loo, in the supermarket, in all the glamorous hot spots. Often I get ideas in my sleep and wake up and tap them into my phone. Then I have to jot that idea down and it makes it into – wait for it – the "Big Fat Greek Mother folder". I'm so incredibly anal and fastidious I amaze myself. I always have so many open tabs in my brain at any one time. Then, weekly I go through to my ever expanding folder and see which idea takes my fancy or more so, which idea jumps up and bites me on my comedy ass.

Then I brainstorm that idea. I'm old school so, I do love me a pen and paper. I even have an old school paper diary. This does cause me problems when I'm out as I can't ever make plans with people until I'm reunited with my weighty doomsday book sized diary. Look I just don't trust phones to remind me to do things. Old lady behaviour like this has sort of just crept up on me damn it! That and also suddenly wincing and announcing in public that I quote unquote "felt a chill". I then stand back and allow my creative scrawlings to ferment like greek yoghurt.

If the concept is still funny after a day or so, well that's that then. That's when I will go ahead and write the sketch in its entirety and then we are going full steam ahead baby! I have to also create a prop list including all the things I will need to make my Spielberg blockbuster. What do I need to shoot this sketch? Where am I shooting? When am I shooting? In the middle of Morrisons again maybe, (a popular haunt) or in my kitchen? If it is in my kitchen I need to clear the surfaces and clear away last night's festering lasagna dish.

Then I have to figure out how many characters I have unhelpfully created for myself to play. What outfits do they need? "Which wig does Carol from accounts fancy?", I'll ask myself. "Oh I'm definitely a short brunette", she replies. What Carol wants, Carol gets. Listen, nobody wants to mess with Carol from accounts.

Finally I shoot the sketch, using my fancy pants ring light, which could take anything from five minutes to five hours depending on its complexity and yet again how ass-kickingly difficult I have decided to make life for myself. Usually it's probably almost always stupendously difficult. At the end there is always a bombsite to clear up, a bit like that poor colourist and their stack of mayhem out back. The chairs go back under the dining table, the massive bookcase gets shifted back, the entire contents of my wardrobe are now piled in a heap on my bed; I think you get the picture. I wonder when I'll ever be minted enough to have a production team, an eager assistant who lives for bringing me soya lattes and doing my post shoot tidy up, but alas no, it's always just muggins. All of that needs to happen before I can even envisage sitting down with a sigh of relief and a cup of tea to actually begin editing the darn thing. Editing by the way is painstaking, you want this video to hit! So you cut out the pauses, speed the action up etc it's a LONG process! Plus the worst bit is having to watch and listen to yourself for the 150th time saying "You'd better get down these stairs young man!" or something equally cringe to that effect. Then you cut to the video colouring stage and the subtitling, hold on we're nearly there Barb don't fall asleep. Then you select some music, if you want it, caption the video and shoot a video cover. PHEW. Then it's over.

Only it's not, You then have to wait to post at peak engagement hour, but the algorithm is a pedantic, temperamental little f****r and you never know if your cherished little video is gonna do well or not. Sometimes the videos I work on for the longest perform the worst, and the ones I shoot off the cuff in poor lighting in two nanoseconds soar. I mean go figure. Content creation is both hugely rewarding and painfully demoralising. Social media can feel like a controlling boyfriend who sometimes treats you well so you keep going back to him, forgetting the times he has treated you like dirt. (It's actually most of the time you narcissistic bastard). I often ask myself if I read English for three years and went on to study drama for a further two for this? "Please God," I pray as I lay awake at night I don't want my tombstone to say;

HERE LAY OLGA,
FAITHFUL MOTHER, FRIEND
AND CONTENT CREATOR.

This was not the grand plan. But three little boys came along and then a breakdown happened. All I had was my phone to create for a virtual audience. An audience I am so grateful for and hugely indebted to. The rest, as they say, is history.

Being a content creator is lonely and isolating. It sometimes feels like there is no off button. I'm constantly scouring the internet sourcing ideas and memes and trending audios. It never stops. You might have posted a great video but then you worry if the next one will do as well. You're only as good as your next video and the one after that and then the one after that. It never ends. I know I look happy and smiling in my fashion shots and I am, but it's usually because I'm fake smiling at an overflowing street bin in the distance. Nobody is that happy all the time unless they are a lunatic. I know many of my fellow content creators feel the same. You don't get to chat with your colleagues by the photocopier. There is no day off or sick pay if you're ill. No one invites you to the staff Christmas party and there is definitely no team away day, though to be fair I'd probably hate to attend either of those two things. If you take time off your engagement drops, your followers drop, the brands turn away and the work drops.

More and more people are experiencing loneliness than ever before in the UK. Social media, whether you work with it or just use it, can leave you talking to hundreds of people, yet feeling completely alone and drained on the inside. Social media can create a false sense of connection and belonging. Online interactions lack the nonverbal cues, physical presence, and emotional intimacy that are crucial to building and maintaining meaningful relationships. You can know hundreds and thousands of people online and be as lonely as an albatross. Social media can leave you feeling inadequate and comparing your lives with others. Friends and family say just put your phone down but how can you do that when it's literally your job. The graft and the loneliness of being a content creator is something that needs to be talked about.

I often get misunderstood, as though social media content creation is all I do. We seem to have gotten over the hump of derogatory connotations, and the self-proclaimed job title "influencer," it would set my teeth on edge. I'm not here to influence. Just saying the word gives me the ick. I can't influence you to wear a certain clothing brand or cut your hair – nor do I want to. I want to inspire you and encourage you and make you feel good. I want my social media to represent the real me.

I'm first and foremost a writer trying to get a show commissioned. But until I get commissioned, writing doesn't pay, so I need to make the watered down sketches to feed my family. I sometimes feel like my page is like a fast food joint, Mcdonald's maybe, churning out highly entertaining, continually fast-moving, relatable sketches. I know it has to be that way to gain traction but deep down I've always wanted to create a longer form in the guise of more meaningful character comedy television scripts and plays.

I'm currently working on a whole myriad of scripts and performances to help me stay on the path to my goals. Firstly I am developing my award winning short *Stavros and Demetra* – a 1980s teen revenge comedy about a young girl who removes all of the school heartthrob and bully's hair.

My first show *El Greco of Hornsey* is also something I have in development. It was the first show I took to Edinburgh and I've been writing, rewriting and pitching it for four years to get it picked up as a television series. My second show *My Big Fat Greek Menopause*, all about navigating those wonderful changes we go through in life, is currently on tour this year. I'm also currently working on a pilot that follows the life of my fake tanned, gum chewing alter ego Androulla and her baby girl Chlamydia.

In addition I also record the *SPLIT ENDS* podcast, alongside hairdressing expert and my friend, Andrew Barton. We interview guests whilst they have their hair done, intertwined with my comedy cameos. Then I have my ongoing charity work which I love.

When I write about all my projects I ask myself genuinely, I am not sure who would be interested in this. As I write everything down it's both affirming to see all I'm doing, yet actually can also make me feel sad to read about all the things I haven't quite accomplished yet. It's a funny one. Seeing yourself exactly where you are and exactly as you are on paper you are more aware of the gaps. But, maybe we should share more about the not quite there yet parts of our lives. Why does everything need to be finished or compartmentalised? Anyone that's ever achieved anything had high mountains to climb and low valleys to wander around in questioning what the point was in everything. Nothing is easy, nothing is overnight. It is clear to me now too, that not everything comes to you when you're young. There are wonderful accomplishments that can only happen as you get older, because maybe only then are you truly ready for them. Maybe in being truthful and in sharing the not quite there yet parts of my life I can encourage others to keep striving for their own dreams and ambitions, no matter the hurdles, no matter the holdbacks. I've known so many rejections and been in so many "almost" scenarios when I thought I'd get commissioned. It's rough, but then I get my head down and keep going. I believe in tenacity and keeping on in the face of constant rejection. Also when I look back and see the things or places I've been rejected from, I've been thankful realising that they were never meant for me. I've often felt relief in hindsight that I was protected from something. All it takes is one yes I tell myself, so don't you dare give up girl.

I'm still working on all of these projects and I recognise that I need the McDonald's content in order to support me financially, so I can get to make the Ottolenghi content. Most comedy creators out there are not solely content creators, they are actors and writers, some have children and are looking for a way to get back to work. I wear so many hats; actor, writer, stand-up comedian but often people only see the one, 'influencer' online. But I am in fact all of those things.

As a side note, please stop thinking content creators get stuff for free. Most of the time it's dumb shit, "Here I'd love to give you this amazing edible keyring that costs £15.99, in exchange for a video and three stories that will take you the best part of three days to make." No thanks you can take your edible keyring, and stick it where the sun doesn't shine. There is no 'free', a brand only wants to give us something in exchange for a feature on our pages. I don't need or want an air purifying unit in exchange for making five videos for your brand. I'll save myself the bother and just open the window. Like many other content creators our pages have not appeared overnight. These are pages many of us have been building day in and day out for over ten years. Many content creators like myself often feel undervalued by agents and brands like we have to prove our worth again and again.

For a long time I kept myself in compartments. Over here I'd be the mother, over here is the wife, over here is the comedian. I was rigid about what I posted, filtering parts of my life, posting things that I thought would only be interesting. Now I see that all of me matters and all of me is interesting. It's a bit like layers really. We all have layers to ourselves. There is so much more than that which we see on the surface. The layers of our lives make us all so wonderfully complex. We are not one-dimensional beings. I'm often asked to do a hair tutorial and I think if I did that, would it belittle me as a writer? No stop this snobbery and overthinking, I tell myself. Think layers. Writers need to do their hair too unless they are so successful they don't have time to fix their hair and get others to do it for them, in which case can I have their secret please?

Pursuing a career in comedy hasn't always been easy. Especially when for a long time social media was my shopfront. I have often been misunderstood or labelled as "too nice" or "annoying". I've been subject to hurtful trolling in the past. I love social media. It has afforded me many opportunities but there is also a dark underbelly to it; jealousy, greed and gossiping about others to make yourself feel better. There are cliques and engagement pods, there is so much that goes on beneath the digital surface.

Can't stand that big fat greek woman jumping about in wigs all day
Who does she think she is?
Her husband and kids must cringe.

Tattle 2019

The hateful language that first poured out against me for no reason online nearly broke me. I was unprepared for it when I first began creating content. I got very ill and anxious in the early days. We had just lost my niece, Grace and it was a very dark time. I remember hovering over the 'delete my account' button on Instagram. I felt so ashamed and projected everything onto myself, that people saw me in this way. That they hated me. Now I see how those comments made me stronger. I will continue to be annoyingly loud and bang my drum of happiness. I've consoled myself by making up names and lives for these sad people who kept themselves anonymous. One of them is called Sue who has a house full of diamante trays with fake Chanel books on it. No wonder she wrote about me. The poor woman is BORED. Also, I actually find these comments quite hilarious now, a source of great entertainment and content!

Your eyebrows look like two slugs

Instagram 2023

You look like old Mother Hubbard 1800s American outback housewife

Facebook 2024

You dance like my grandma

Tiktok 2025

Never give up on your dreams. Your dreams are the most important thing about your life. They make you who you are. No matter how small or insignificant your dreams may seem, don't let them go. I remember friends and family thinking I'd lost the plot when I started posting online. One well-meaning friend even told me to maybe think of what I was doing as a hobby rather than a legitimate career. Relatives were concerned about my bizarre online antics. But now they see the fruits of the belief I had in myself and they love to cheer me on. Not everyone is going to clap for you, so clap for yourself. Don't wait for anyone's permission or approval. Take those little steps every day to get closer to making that dream a reality. Believe in yourself, you have everything going for you and if you're still struggling to do that, well, I believe in you.

15

CHOPPY

Θα φας ξύλο
You will eat wood!

A choppy hairstyle is achieved when sections of hair are divided and cut down in a random way. The stylist cuts your hair in asymmetrical, layered portions to create a blunt, edgy texture. Forget your pretty polished hairstyle. This is something different. It looks chaotic at first but as all the sections come together the effect gives the hair beautiful shape and movement.

Choppy water is water that is rippled, full of small waves caused by strong winds. It can also be described as lumpy, bumpy, or messy, with the water surface moving up and down and side to side. Choppy water is often seen during storms. Choppy can also be used as an idiom to refer to difficult, uncertain, or troublesome times. For example, you might say "We are passing through choppy waters" when experiencing tough times.

Once a struggle has passed, you won't look back at it and feel the pain you did when you were going through it. Bad times will end, and you will feel better. There is a saying "It's sweet to see the sea from the land when you don't have to sail any longer." I'm in a calm settled space now and the waters are still. But whenever I find myself struggling I have to go back and rewind the years to have a little talk with that little scared immigrant girl who felt outcast and ridiculed. I have to take her and sit her on my knee and settle her down. She gets fractious and unsettled sometimes, speeding up when she needs to slow down.

I have to remind her that she is no longer unwanted. I've had years of counselling to unlearn people-pleasing because of the bullying I went through. I've had to teach myself not to always pacify the needs of others. It's been an arduously long journey, I've had to let people go whose happiness depended on whether I kept them on side. It's funny isn't it how when you start showing some people the same strength they show you they don't like it. Interestingly enough I found my circle became smaller the taller and more confident I became.

I was tired of playing a game of waiting for certain people's signals of approval or disapproval. I stopped playing the role of peace-maker, middleman and moderator. I was not responsible for people's own contentment with life. I used to broil in resentment and fantasise about whether others were pleased with me or not. I would analyse and study their text responses to see if they were angry with me or if I was still lucky enough to be in their good books. I would find myself completely undone by someone else's behaviour towards me.

I didn't fit into some people's boxes anymore and they didn't like it and those relationships ended.

Today I am freer and stronger. I will keep on telling my story again and again because I know it helps others. Because there is bravery in vulnerability and strength in embracing our weakness. You see like so many, many children out there today, I now know I was picked on back then not just because I was different, but because I was so amazingly special.

Many adults who were bullied as children often suffer lasting emotional and psychological effects. Many experience low self-esteem, anxiety, depression, anger issues, and difficulty forming relationships, but many of these adults have managed to overcome their past trauma and lead successful lives. It has been shown that years after being mistreated, some people with adult post-bullying syndrome commonly struggle with trust and self-esteem, and can develop psychiatric problems. Some become people-pleasers or rely on food, alcohol, or drugs to cope. People who had been bullied tended to have less education and fewer qualifications by age 50 than those who were never bullied. There have been many negative ramifications in my life because of the school playground, but I refused to become a statistic. I turned my life around and overcame many of the traumatic experiences that happened to me. The hangover of being the chubby bullied kid at school who didn't speak any English is finally over for me. I'm so proud to reclaim that ground as an ambassador for Kidscape, an anti-bullying charity who are there to support young people and their families. It's the greatest honour of my life. Kidscape's vision is for all children to grow up in supportive communities, safe from bullying and harm.

When I first started my Instagram account way back in the tech dark ages I would never in a million years have dreamed of being where I am now. I'm here. I'm not hiding. I genuinely don't care what anyone thinks of me. Especially from someone who doesn't know me, and chooses to spread hate because their lives are so empty and sad.

When people say unkind things it's more a reflection on their own unhappiness. I know I'm not for everyone. The aforementioned trolls have eagerly pointed this out to me in the past. But guess what, we were never made to please everyone. It's mind numbingly boring and ever so exhausting. Even if you were perfect people would still pick holes. I'm not going to change to make myself popular like I tried to do when I was a kid. No, this is it. Finally, I think I like who I am. There came a point where I had to be brave and say "this is me" and take my space.

Research shows that bullying is corrosive to children's mental health and wellbeing, with consequences ranging from trouble sleeping and skipping school to psychiatric problems, such as depression or psychosis, self-harm, and suicide. But with Kidscape no one has to face bullying alone. I'm currently developing a documentary film called *Speaking with Myself* exploring the story of my journey, from bullied outcast kid to a comedian and ambassador for the charity. Back in the '80s and '90s my parents were not given a definition of what bullying was, it wasn't something that we were taught about. There wasn't the information or the help I needed. I love this charity with all my heart. Supporting them today is my way of seeing everything that was taken from me restored, poured into the lives of others. Here are a few words from the charity's Chief Executive.

"We are very thankful and grateful to our Kidscape ambassadors who use their own profiles to raise awareness of bullying, its impact and the support available to those who experience bullying. Olga Thompson has bravely shared her own childhood experiences of bullying at school, all because she stood out and was different. That very difference is what makes Olga unique, talented and gifted as an Actor, Singer, Comedian and Author. She is a very special ambassador.

Always remember, no matter what, there is never an excuse for bullying, and you are not to blame. Being different is a valuable gift to cherish and celebrate, bullying does not define you, your personality will always be yours to keep."

Paula Timms Chief Executive Kidscape

When you next feel anxious or running scared try and speak to yourself like you would a little child. I have had to do a lot of work on myself in counselling these past thirty years to find that peace within myself. They say the most contented people are those who have made peace with their inner child. I have found this to be true. In fact, if I ever find myself feeling stuck or blocked in life I have to come back to that little 6-year-old girl and reassure her, in order to be able to move forward. Being gentle with yourself is important because adulting is actually really hard and sometimes it can feel like we are all playing these big grown up roles. Speak the words you never heard as a child, but desperately needed to hear. Take time out if you need it and be kind to yourself and to that little person within you. The waters will settle soon enough.

16
THINNING

Είσαι τούβλο.
You're a brick.

We can lose between 50 and 100 hairs a day, often without even noticing. Hair loss is not usually anything to be worried about. Seasonal hair shedding begins in the summer and usually peaks in the autumn. Ready for the science-y bit? Your hair growth cycle involves three different phases — the anagen phase (or growth phase), the catagen phase (or transition phase) and the telogen phase (or resting phase). In the third, the telogen phase, it's totally normal for hair to naturally shed, so that the follicle can start the cycle all over again. This phase of the hair cycle lasts about three months. It's normal, but occasionally it can be a sign of a medical condition. I'm used to this cycle every year without fail and it's always been ok; until it wasn't.

My Mama always had beautiful thick hair and wore it in glamorous, blonde, blow dried curls down past her shoulders. She showed us how to slather our hair with olive oil to keep it thick and shiny. Over the years I loved having hair I could manipulate into any hairstyle I wanted. It was sturdy, strong obedient hair. It was compliant, receptive to perm lotions and hair dyes, red, blonde, blue-black it happily lapped up all the colours. My Mama always told everyone that "Olga she have the strong hair". I had good hair and this was my accolade and my trophy. It had never failed me.

I noticed in the summer of 2022 that I was losing a bit more hair than usual. It was starting to fall everywhere; on my pillow, on the floors. I knew something wasn't right but I was in denial. My hair had been my comforter, the one thing I could rely on; the idea that it was falling away from me was devastating. I just couldn't bring myself to face it was happening. It was only when Paul appeared one day with handfuls of my hair he had rooted out of the shower plug hole, that the cold truth presented itself to me. I couldn't bear to look at myself in the mirror, as I noticed the light bouncing off my thinning hairline revealing more and more of my scalp. My scalp line was slowly receding, I was inconsolable. My strands were lacklustre, dry and brittle and breaking off, I also noticed my eyebrows had started to become sparse and thin. It was apparent even in the videos I made online and I'd find myself shooting myself from below so you couldn't see my thinning hair. I felt so ugly and depressed. I'd also noticed around the time that I was putting on weight, every inch of me felt achy and swollen. I was permanently exhausted. I couldn't figure out what on earth was wrong with me.

I kept returning to the doctors again and again only to be told it was probably just menopause. But I knew deep down it wasn't. Eventually hospital blood tests revealed I had Hashimoto's, an underactive thyroid. I broke down in tears that I eventually had a diagnosis. The thyroid gland is butterfly-shaped and is found in the front of your neck, it's like a tiny thermostat that regulates your whole body. My immune system which usually fights infection had attacked my thyroid gland and damaged it, which meant it was unable to make enough of the hormone thyroxine. When hormone production is disrupted, it affects other processes in the body. This includes the development of hair at the root. Hair falls out resulting in thinning across the scalp and other areas. This also led to me having problems such as fatigue, brittle nails and depression. I also noticed puffiness in my face and suffered muscle cramps and digestive problems as my metabolism slowed down. I also found myself feeling permanently tired all the time even after eight hours of sleep. Going up the stairs felt like climbing a mountain. With low thyroid hormone, metabolism slows down and it can feel like your body grinds to a halt.

It was a nightmare finding the root cause for all the problems I was having. Symptoms of an underactive thyroid are often very similar to those of other conditions so can be tricky to diagnose, they usually develop slowly, so you may not notice them for years. For many women who may be suffering symptoms which make them feel they have started the menopause it could actually be that of an underactive thyroid. It's also not unusual for midlife women going through perimenopause to also have a thyroid condition. As symptoms often overlap, it can be difficult to establish which are related to the thyroid and which to perimenopause.

It was one of the worst periods of my life, as someone who makes a living putting up videos of herself online; I wanted to hide from the world. I would wash my hair without touching it so as to protect myself from seeing the hair fall out. I would close my eyes as I brushed it and then give the comb to my husband to dispose of the hair in a bag so I wouldn't see it. I felt bereft. Eventually I avoided washing it or even touching it altogether. I disassociated myself from it as though it was no longer a part of me, like a hat I could remove at any moment. It was detached from me, it was other. I still feel traumatised by that time. Hair has a profoundly magical influence on human emotions. Thick, beautiful hair, is linked to self-identity and has nothing to do with vanity. Whether good or bad, hair is inescapably connected with how you view yourself. Losing your hair causes a significant shift that can shake you to your core. Hair is called one's crowning glory because it symbolises one's personality. It's no surprise then that for me losing that symbol took a real toll on my self-esteem. For me my hair loss was a loss. It unearthed a deep grief, a sorrow within me. My hair was something I hid behind even when I felt at my ugliest. My hair would never fail me and would somehow make up for what I felt I lacked. Now I had no safety blanket. I felt exposed and vulnerable.

It's taken two years of doctors' appointments and medication doses being raised and lowered for my body to adjust and settle. I've cut gluten, wheat, alcohol and caffeine (tragic I know) from my diet – all of which I have found can affect the absorption of my meds. It's been a long road but my bloods are even and my body is finally responding to the medication in the way it's supposed to. I feel I'm back and my lovely thick hair is back too. Maybe this is why I refuse to keep it short. I'm indulging in it, cherishing every strand. In fact I'm considering growing it so crazily long that when I'm an old lady I can sit on it in my rocking chair. It's mine, all of it. I cherish it and no one can ever take it away from me again.

If you feel something isn't right in your body, always get it checked out. Trust yourself. Be persistent. Don't stop asking health professionals until you get the answers you need. Sometimes it's trial and error, sometimes it takes time but you are worth it. Don't fear health screenings; they are important, especially if there is a family history related illness. It turned out thyroid conditions ran in my family. These checks could save your life. I'm so glad I listened to my body and persisted back and forth with the doctors to get the right diagnosis and medication dosage that I needed. Sometimes we keep on going for everyone else around us and it's easy to neglect our own needs. Try to listen to your body and nurture it. You would feed your child fruit and vegetables, so why do we often fail to feed ourselves with the good stuff? Watch your stress levels and check your alcohol intake. Oh and make sure you are watering yourself as much as you do those plants (guilty). Get outside even in winter, fresh air helps everything feel better and make sure you're getting enough sleep too. Take the time to do the things that make you feel good.

17

SHE BANGS SHE BANGS

Ἔριξε μαύρη πέτρα πίσω της.
She threw a black rock over her shoulder.

Aside from my obsession with hair, I've always been fascinated by clothes. Inspired by watching my parents flamboyant style and fashionable flair even in the face of adversity, I understood from an early age that clothing signified status and power. Clothes and fashion gave you a ticket to wherever you wanted to go and permission to be whoever you wanted to be. The power clothes can bestow has always fascinated me, not only when it comes to sourcing costumes and dressing my characters but for myself also. Over the years dressing up as someone else has helped me deal with my mental health demons. Clothes can be powerful, a mask, a comfort, an armour, a signifier. Clothes can heal and they can bind. Clothes can bring you home.

Whilst I do like shopping online and on the highstreet, I've always loved the thrill of a charity shop and thrift stores, you never know the jewels you are going to find. My favourite pieces are items that could have been worn by your uncle on his way to a card game in the '80s. The wonderful thing about wearing vintage clothes is that you know for sure that you won't turn up at an event with someone in the same frock as you. My style staples were always a vintage print dress and a good set of trainers, accessorised by lots of '80s junk gold. Finished off of course with my signature 'Lady Danger' Mac lip. My trainers are non-negotiable and always keep me rooted no matter how "out there" my dress might be. I love following trends but then finding ways to source those items myself in thrift shops. More than anything though, I love the way these clothes tell stories.

Having grown up in the '80s that's the era that has stuck with me the most. Make way for power dressing, the obsession with boxy shoulder pads has never and may never leave me. In fact I think my fixation is growing, as too are the shoulder pads. During that time, more was more and anything went. New romanticism, athleisure, secretary look, punk glam. You could be whoever you wanted to be or in fact, you could be a mashup of all of these looks and personas, all at once! For me it was always Lady Diana chic dresses and power blazers for the win. She was an icon. The cobalt blue Cojana suit with a white pussy-bow blouse she wore to stroll the grounds of Buckingham Palace during the announcement of her engagement to Prince Charles will stay forever imprinted on my memory. I remember having a commemorative mirror in my bedroom of Charles and Di on their engagement. I imagined that if I gazed into the mirror long enough I would somehow absorb some of her beauty and elegance. Princess Diana's style was legendary, her looks were so renowned that they even had special names and stories all of their own: the revenge dress, the Travolta dress, the fairytale David and Elizabeth Emmanuel wedding dress. Each stands out as a distinct, lasting pop culture moment. Diana was an inspiration to millions for both her philanthropic work and her distinctive personal expression. Growing up she was an icon to me. I adored her, truly.

For the many years when I lost myself due to my breakdown, clothes were a way of finding myself again. A way to be creative and to play. I began to care about myself and my body, how I dressed it, fed it and clothed it. Fashion was a way to reconnect with myself and the world around me. Fashion for me has always felt like theatre. A way to create a daily stage all of my own. A way of setting myself apart.

Ever since I was a little girl, I've always loved dressing up. Trying on my Mama's fabulous dresses led to a fascination with costume and a love of theatre. Clothes spoke something deep into my being, they helped to make sense of the things in the world that both troubled and perplexed me. In the darkest of days clothes were a way of signalling hope that better days were coming. Fashion and mental health, two seemingly separate spheres criss-crossing, lending to one another. Fashion is more than just a means of adorning the body; it is a powerful form of self-expression that reflects identity, mood, and personal values. When I was struggling with depression, getting dressed, wearing clean clothing, and washing my face felt massive. Doing those things gave me some normality and some semblance of control. For me fashion has always gone beyond getting dressed; it's been a way for me to express my creativity, and my longing to be seen. Fashion has and always will be a physical reminder to myself that I matter.

Just as I love experimenting with clothes for myself, I'm lucky to have the pleasure of looking for outfits and creating styles for all my zany characters too. I can't tell you the freedom of playing Bambos, an adult overgrown toddler, a pampered pooch that lives with his mum. He wears comfy football kits topped off with women's dressing gowns, day and night and honestly, I'm here for it. He loves the freedom those airy shorts give his crown jewels.

I always workshop my characters and play with movement and voice. How does it feel to be in their shoes? Are they larger or smaller than me? How does their skin feel? How do they walk? What do they wear when it's cold? Do they wear heels? What about a hat? I dress them according to their personalities and it's a riot.

Aunty Fanoulla favours large elasticated pants for easy squatting and comfortable no nonsense lady sandals with a thermal sock for her hop on bus rides. But Androulla likes everything nipped in, shiny and tight for her daily girl boss Instagram posts and fancy lunches at Subway. If it's leopard print or mock croc she's bagging it. The best part is going shopping in character and selecting things they might like. I will speak to myself in their voices "Ooh that's nice for bingo, stretchy good ones" grunts Aunty Fanoulla pulling out some fisherman's trousers. "Stavvy's eyes are gonna pop out when he sees these wet look jeggings and sparkly boob tube!" squeals Androulla. I wander round shops muttering their voices to myself quietly under my breath so as to avoid getting strange stares or even worse, removed by security. At home of course I'm not so inhibited. The boys have grown up seeing their mother dress up and play different characters around the house for years and are used to it. In fact they are unphased. I have a photo of Bambos at Christmas with two of my boys, little, sitting on his lap. They have grown up with all my characters, it's like they are part of the family now. Meeting Bambos by the microwave wearing their dad's y-fronts and vest doesn't even make them flinch these days. Mind you they are teens, so they are at that time of life where nothing much makes them flinch, but the eye rolls... oh the eye rolls are off the charts.

When it comes to me however, I've found as I've gotten older, I've gotten to know myself better too. My style has changed, evolved and softened. It's more effortless and laid back. I no longer need clothes to speak boldly for me, to announce my arrival, to make me stand out from the crowd. I know who I am now, so my clothes are just an extension of that. I no longer need them to give me an identity but rather to enhance who I already am. I feel comfortable in my own skin and I need my clothes to be an expression of that. I wear more tailored, relaxed pieces these days and the Lady Di vintage dresses are still there of course, but the colours are softer and the eclectic prints have been absorbed by sober stripes and low key patterns. I enjoy mixing both vintage and modern clothes today and get my playtime that way. I'm kinder to my body and I'm more considerate in the way I choose to dress it. I love that vintage clothes are sustainable and kinder to our planet. These days I favour breathable, ethically made sustainable pieces. I much prefer to invest in something that will last rather than something that will be thrown away tomorrow. I buy less and hang on to my clothes more. My style breathes a lot more these days, it kind of flows, as do I.

For a long time I was editing myself. What I wore and how I appeared. What I posted and how I posted. I wore different hats for different occasions. Now thankfully I've ditched all the hats apart from my wooly green beanie that makes me look like a stocky farmhand. I'm who I am and there is so much more to me and I don't need to shoehorn myself anywhere to make myself more palatable to others. This is me just as I am. I'm complex, yes, but I don't owe anyone an explanation anymore and neither do you.

At the risk of sounding like a segment on This Morning don't be afraid to have your own style. Embracing your own unique flair is empowering and allows you to express yourself truthfully and authentically. Never feel pressured to look or be like anyone else. That would be most sad and hugely boring if we all dressed the same because we would never get to see you and all your gorgeousness. Style is personal, you can be as extreme or minimalist as you like. Ditch the fear of what people will think of you and if you want to wear the shoulder pads, then wear the damn shoulder pads.

18

DUCKS ARSES

Σιγά τα λάχανα.
Slowly the cabbage.

When I was young I would watch my Mama give that one signature hairstyle to every single woman over 40. It was a defining blowdry that said "Lady you're fast approaching the death knell of midlife so here have a duck's arse hairstyle on us". Let me explain. The hair would be cut short ("because well, you're getting on a bit love, so no tumbling locks for you") then curled, blow dried and teased with a hairdryer and round brush to create a duck's arse effect. My Mama would then proceed to backcomb the hair around the sides, and part it centrally down the back of the head.

The ducktail, or duck's arse, was a popular men's look in the 1940s and '50s. The Ducktail style, unsurprisingly, got its name from the resemblance to a duck's side-swept backside. Nice. So duck's arse-ishingly convincing was the style that I would wait wide-eyed in the expectation of an egg coming out of the back of the over-forty-something customer's hair!

You knew you were one step closer to the grave, you old hag you, when you got given a duck's arse blow dry. But nowadays, for me there's only one thing worse, than the 'D.A blow dry', A F*****G-CLUCKING fascinator that's what!! This is the modern over-40 woman's announcement to the world that she has totally lost all sense of identity and there is nothing for it, but to stick a giant dirty great big bird on her head. It's like hey, I know I'm no longer youthful, so I'm just gonna letcha know I'm still here ok, rocking this sizable, stuffed, multicoloured pigeon on my head.

I literally loathe the fascinator section of department stores, I avert my eyes and scurry past as quickly as I can, hearing the garishly bitchy caps mocking and calling out to me "Come join us you old bag, stick one of us on your head, come on don't fight it any longer."

No. No no no no no. It ain't ever gonna happen. Even when I'm senile and 87, sat in a care home and slurping my own urine out of a sippy cup, I will insist on permanently wearing (whilst still cognitive) a t-shirt that says "NO F*****G FASCINATORS". Look, it's truthfully not just about the fascinator itself, if you feel great in one then go for it, it's just I'm tired of women being made to feel like they need to disappear off the face of the earth when they hit 40. It's like society panics us into wearing fascinators and breathable lame, lime, floral two pieces and comfortable, fleece lined, velcro strapped, slip-on shoes from a particular brand from hell (I can't name) which may or may not sound like trotters. Also don't insult me. I'm never buying elasticated skirts that look like they've been made out of sofa fabrics out the back of some Sunday newspaper supplement. I'd rather go stark bollock naked with my hoochy coochy on show.

I hate the way fashion polarises older women. It's either tan tights, granny with comfortable shoes on a coach trip to Clacton crossed with daytime TV presenter, or Britney circa 2006. Our fashion brains haven't fallen out of our bottoms. We are cleverer and cooler than you give us credit for. Big corporations have mostly been run by men and used as a stick to hit us with or to make us spend money on age defying toot and eye watering fashion we don't need, or that make us feel like we have to stay young. Anti-ageing is a sinister money making enterprise stemming from patriarchy. Let's refuse it and stick it in the bin. I think pro-age is a much nicer way to go don't you?

Brands are the worst culprits. Aiming their fashion at younger women when we "older women" are the ones with the disposable income. Our kids, if we have them, have grown up, we are more settled and have the time and money to buy clothes. It's exhausting and it's polarising. What if I don't want to dress like a teenager or a hag? Is there any middle ground for me? What if I just want to dress like me? Why do we need "Over-fifty fashion" like we have suddenly become dribbling and incompetent and need to be led over to the breathable lime two-pieces section. Which by the way is always handily situated next to the fascinators so they CAN TRAP YOU! My fashion brains haven't fallen out of my duck's arse. Give me some credit. I'm still here. I'm still me. Treat me with some respect damn it.

Another thing. Just because I talk about menopause and getting older doesn't mean that that is my whole vibe. Look, I'm allowed to talk about menopause without it becoming my whole personality type. I'm so weary of being offered indigestion tablets jobs or support pants campaigns just because of my age. I still love fashion. I still read, eat out and I still like nice things. My whole life isn't just about suppositories and neck creams. It's painfully dull and exhausting. I'm so tired of being ignored. Women ten years younger than me are being offered fancy high street fashion brands and I am over here being offered vulva tightening creams. Listen, I will never wear velcro comfortable trainers. I'm not dead yet. Would you like me to be?

Another thing we are bombarded by, pro-ageing skincare products and information, but it feels like the hair industry needs to catch up. Have you thought about your hair? Refuse to disappear, refuse to let your hair go. Wash it, love it, nurture it as you would yourself. If dyeing your hair makes you feel good, do it! If you want to wear it beautifully grey do it. But please look after your grey, it also needs special care, love and upkeep. Women over 40 don't neglect your hair, It's your crowning glory. Care for it as you do every part of your body. When was the last time you went to the hairdresser, or even just gave yourself a little deep conditioning treatment at home? Brushing or massaging your scalp can be incredibly therapeutic.

Also for the record all this immediately having to cut your hair short when you hit forty fad is nonsense. That dull old premise – that women of a certain age should not wear their hair long – has no place or relevance anymore. Long hair, should you want to wear it that way, after a certain age is beautiful, a statement stopping you from disappearing or being ignored. Here's a quote from my good friend Andrew Barton, celebrity hairdresser, on why women shouldn't be afraid of having longer hair as they get older:

"I'm often asked if there is an age when a woman should cut off her locks. Of course it's a personal choice but I've never been an advocate of a woman doing it just because she is of a certain age. In fact, when so much else changes in her life associated around ageing, why would she cut her hair off? It is something that makes her feel feminine and her long hair is part of her ID. For many women hair is not just part of her physical appearance but part of her sense of wellbeing, it's her crowning glory. The secret to wearing hair longer whatever your age is to wear it well cut and shaped, with a little movement and shining with health and vitality."

Andrew Barton 'The Hair Expert'

See, long hair over 50 does not mean I'm one of the witches in Macbeth or Neil from *The Young Ones!* As I've gotten older my hair has gotten longer and I have no intention of cutting it. No, I'm not tempted by Daily Mail articles telling me I must cut myself a short lady bob at "my age" to stay young looking.

Yawn. Those same irrelevant articles also tell me it's a good idea to always have to match my bag and my shoes. Also do not mention "waist cinching", "chic" or "glam" to me as I approach 50 as I will literally break out in hives.

My hair is longer than it's ever been. I'm wearing a softer style, flowing loose and carefree, a bit like me. I'm less bothered by peer pressure, I'm far more confident these days to do my own thing with my hair. It's my hair and I will wear it how I want. Long hair after a certain age I believe can give you a presence, it stops the invisible cloak from descending. It's a distinctive feature which as we age prevents us, consciously or otherwise, from disappearing.

I'm a bonafide midlife crew member. I embrace it all, apart from those terrible sun life insurance adverts on television with wooden actors in chintzy kitchens positively delirious with joy at having to plan their own funerals. "Ooh I'll have such peace of mind knowing that when I get mauled by a rogue combine harvester in Somerset next June, that my family will receive a substantial payout. Another custard cream Ken?" I'm an older woman now but I refuse to be swept under the carpet, erased like a bad drawing. I know what I look like. What am I supposed to do, stop ageing? Disappear? I'd love it if just for once the supermarket assistant would actually look at me to see if I was over 18 whilst purchasing alcohol at the express checkout. Don't just look at the back of me, I scream in my head clutching my reusable shopper, don't just assess me by my barrelled silhouette and drooping derrière!! Please actually look at me. Believe me you would be surprised at how I actually look 26 from the front, if you were standing ten metres away, in the dark and squinting. Look, seriously now, I don't want to be younger, I just want to be seen. Hello world, look at me, look at all my beautiful flaws and bumps and wrinkles and all. Can I get an Amen?

When women stop me in the street or send me DMs that they connect with my comedy it literally lights me up. It's so rewarding when other women say they see themselves in me. Neither of us are alone, I validate them but they validate me too with their words of encouragement. Sometimes I don't feel confident about my body and the way things are changing. Sometimes I feel as funny as wart cream. I want to hide but I choose not to because I know there are so many women out there feeling just like me. So I choose to show up for them so they can see themselves reflected back on the screen. I refuse to stay silent for them. When I get seen, we all get seen. Every single, damn, hot flushing one of us. Duck's arse blow dry mentality? Do one!

Refuse to conform to someone else's expectation for your life. Even mine in this book. Wear your hair and your clothes how you want. Society is very quick to tell us what we should look, feel and be like after 40. Never compromise. Never apologise. Focus on what makes you truly happy, not on pleasing others. Your worth is not determined by other people's acceptance. Embrace your strengths, your unique abilities and talents. Refuse to let others tell you who you are. Remember that what people think of you is actually really just a reflection of themselves, not you. You can't control other people's thoughts and opinions about you. It's like chasing the wind. All you can do is be happy with being your own, wonderful self. Wear the clothes you want and rock the hair you want. Say no to the pressure and definitely say no to the duck's arses blow dry, well unless you really want one that is.

19

BY APPOINTMENT ONLY

Μια αστραπή η ζωή μας, μα προλαβαίνουμε.
Our life is like lightning, but we're
catching up.

My Mama had a "By Appointments Only" sign in her hairdressing shop window. My Baba thought it a good idea to deter people from wandering in off the street wanting their hair done whenever they felt like it. We also had a massive, brown, beaten, leather bound appointments book for writing down customers' timings.

Each customer had a specific day or time they liked to come. All the Greek customers would congregate on a Saturday to see each other and have a gossip over a Greek coffee. The older English ladies liked coming midweek when it was quieter on pensioner days for their wash and blue rinse sets.

And of course, we had the young women coming in on Friday nights for their blow drys ahead of their big nights out. People are creatures of habit really, a bit like always sitting in the same spot when you go to church, or when you like to go food shopping, or where you sit in the waiting room when you visit the doctors. I always like to perch myself by the herpes poster. Everyone had a set appointed time at the salon and they stuck to it. Well then once I hit middle age, I figured maybe my appointed time in life is now.

Did you know Greeks have two words for time: Chronos (χρόνος) and Kairos (καιρός). Kairos is an ancient Greek word meaning seasons and the perfect timing of things; Chronos refers to tick-tock chronological time. Chronos is the measure of quantitative time, more specifically exact time. Chronos is the forward propelling time that we measure with clocks, on our phones, on watches, and by the evolutionary phases of the moon. But time does not end there.

I have been thinking a lot about how we get so caught up in a clock watching way of living that we stop measuring moments and instead measure seconds. If something doesn't happen right away we want to give up, right? It's a stressful way to live. Not if you pay attention to Kairos. Kairos speaks about opportunity and favour, occasions and grace. Kairos, is qualitative time or "Deep Time", an experience where our perception of Chronos stops or disappears, and we're able to be free to be truly present. It is a gift to ourselves when we recognize these precious kairological moments in our lives and relish them. Kairos moments are those rich things that cannot be measured — community, nature, family and celebration.

Did you know there is such a thing as Chronophobia, an extreme fear of time or the passage of time. People with this anxiety disorder feel intense discomfort or dread when they think about time passing them by. They obsess about their own mortality or worry about getting older. Some people become obsessed with watching the clock or marking days off the calendar. Chronophobia can cause people to have racing thoughts or obsessive behaviours. In severe cases, it can lead to panic attacks, social isolation and problems with relationships.

Kairos tells us that regardless of lateral time and years our dreams will still come true and that which is for us will not pass us by. So don't give up and keep holding onto your hope because your time will come. Give yourself permission to see that your life has always been in seasons not seconds. Without winter you cannot have spring. There have been some dark and painful roads I have walked without which I wouldn't have appreciated the ushering in of the light. I am learning to embrace Kairos and a more meaningful, qualitative way of living where I am, moving forward in my own time and my own way. I am not rushing. I don't need or want to be where anyone else is. I am open, ready to experience the wonderful things that were always intended for me. So never give up because great things are coming; they just might take Kairos, not Chronos time.

If you're like me it's easy to lose heart when you feel like you've been waiting a long time on things. Life doesn't always go the way you want it to. It always seems to spoil my carefully executed plans and do its own thing anyway. It's crushing isn't it? It's inevitable that life will bring sorrow and pain, trials and tribulations. But you need to remember that 'this too shall pass' relates to everything we go through. Nothing stays the same. At some point night will turn into day, mourning into dancing. There is a season just ahead of breakthrough and laughter. All manner of life brings restoration in its own way, and in its own good time. So please be encouraged that all of life's experiences, good and bad, can be categorised into your own appointed timing. There is a beautiful path to follow which is yours and yours alone. Whatever the season, I really want to encourage you today to trust in that. It won't always make sense, believe me I know, but trust the process, It will come good for you.

My Mama always tells us the story about why she became a hairdresser. As one of ten, her father didn't have enough money to send her off to study like her other brothers and sisters who went on to become councillors and architects, so her lot fell to her to become a hairdresser. She bought her first stand-alone hair dryer unit at just 16. She felt nervous starting out, but looking back she says it was the best thing that could have happened to her. She says going into hairdressing meant she always had money in her hands and she was always respected. My Mama's work clothed us and fed us and supported us all these years. It was a profession that enabled me to go to university, a profession that gave her identity and belonging. She often tells us that even though she didn't have an education she was educated in life. This is true. I would decorate her with a thousand honours for the woman of grace and dignity she was and still is. I thank God for my Mama's precious dye stained fingers, deeply riddled today with arthritis, for the sacrifice and love she gave for us.

Things didn't work out for her as she had initially thought they would, but she says they turned out the way they were supposed to. She tells me as I write this, that the difficult times brought her to a place of peace and contentment in her life. "I suffered, yes, but God was always with me and he gave me you, my three precious children. Tell me what more do I want?" Life wasn't easy for her but she nobly walked ahead and I watched from the wings and followed her example.

Life is sweeter for all the pain I've been through. I catch myself sometimes laughing in the garden sunshine with my sons and think these are the greatest days of our lives. Or maybe I'm watching a movie I love and I get lost in it. This is a small thing I know but I'm always grateful when I catch myself enjoying life because there was a time I didn't. Nothing in my life was ever too late, but right on time for me. I feel like things have happened later for me in life. Nothing has been instant but I feel content knowing I am exactly where I am meant to be. Having older children now and going through menopause has funnily enough given me my moment and also exceptional comedy material. You try slathering your inner thighs with freezing cold HRT gel whilst you walk around your room like a penguin waiting for it to dry. I wonder where that feeling of being late in life comes from anyway? Is it really the true picture or is it just society's expectation of us? Is it the demands we and others place on ourselves? I have taught myself that the things I thought were delays in life were actually veiled blessings that steered me to wonderful new places. I have had to stop and ask myself "Woman what exactly do you think you are late for?"

There is an opportune moment and a perfect season for each one of us. For all your worrying and planning you can't make things happen any quicker. Stop watching the relentless tick-tock of the clock. The urge to refresh your inbox every five minutes, just in case that notification hasn't arrived yet. Resist the feeling that the minutes are crawling by, dragging you down with them. This feeling of time imprisonment can kill your passion and your productivity. It fuels negativity and drains your focus. Focus on the amazing progress you have made rather than fixating on time. You, your talents and capabilities are not defined by a clock. If you need to take your watch off, set your phone to aeroplane mode, and silence your calendar. Be more open to Kairos moments, and you'll be more likely to experience them. Connect to your surroundings, to nature, and to the people beside you. All of a sudden there is no longer the manic hurry and crazed rush, you permit yourself to drop your shoulders, sit back and take a deep breath and realise that you are exactly where you are supposed to be.

20

THE SANCTUARY OF THE HAIRDRESSING CHAIR

Κράτα με θα σε κρατήσω να ανέβουμε στο βουνό.
Hold my hand and I'll hold yours so we can
climb the mountain.

Hairdressers are more than just hairdressers, they are counsellors, helpers, encouragers, confidants, psychologists and advisors. Surely we all know that a visit to your hairdresser is about more than just having your hair done. It makes you feel good inside and out. You get to know your hairdresser and your hairdresser gets to know you. It's quite an intimate exchange, one that involves degrees of touch and care. After covid it was the hairdressers who were the real heroes. We needed them to rectify all the botched DIY haircuts we had inflicted on ourselves in desperation during social distancing. We had missed them and we had missed the way they had made our hair look and feel. Also for many people it was emotional to have such proximity to another individual again after months of lockdown and isolation. For many people on their own who hadn't had human contact in many months, returning to the hairdressers and having that human touch again by their hairdresser's hands was hugely emotional.

Over the years, I saw how my Mama loved and counselled her customers, she genuinely cared for them and they for her. They became her friends. Many of them told her their deepest darkest secrets. The hairdressing chair was a safe place, a stand-alone place where they could bear their souls. A place where they could be undisturbed by the demands of other people, a place where they could come away and analyse and release their burdens and cares. In many ways a hairdressing chair is like a counsellor's chair. It carries that same power, that very same weight to it. We all need someone that we can completely share our innermost thoughts and emotions with don't we? Talking with friends and family can be helpful, but often we don't speak honestly and openly about our deepest feelings with those who are the closest to us. I've been open about my mental health struggles and how I've coped. Counselling has been hugely instrumental in helping me to recover. Every decade or so I seem to find myself in a place where I need to talk and unburden myself of deep things. Things that I don't fully understand myself and neither would I be able to share with those around me. A bit like a massive house clearout where we get rid of clutter and junk that doesn't serve us anymore. At those moments I find the need to unburden myself of the things I can no longer carry forward with me into the next season. It always starts with that sensation of feeling stuck with a huge weight bearing down on my chest that I can't shift. Talking with a trained professional has always helped me to make sense of things and heal from past traumas. Often we see getting help or going for counselling as a negative thing. As though we have something wrong with us so we feel ashamed. But why? We aren't robots. We are not machines that function like clockwork. Also, let's remember, machines break down too, and we allow for that fact and understand that we need to fix them sometimes. Why then, can we extend this grace to machinery but not to our own living breathing selves? I actually feel that the most well adjusted people I know, the ones who are comfortable in their own skin, the ones who seem to really know themselves, are the ones who have been open to talking therapies. By the way, for the record, it doesn't mean "in therapy good", "not in therapy bad". It just means if you need it, it's ok to go. There is a long way to go to destigmatize this.

My growth by the way and for the record, has always been slow and measured. Everything feels like it took its time, slow and laboured. I think it's like that for most people actually, and we would know that, if people felt like they could speak freely and honestly about it.

Growth is laborious, steady and unseen. It can be dark and lonely, sometimes boring and repetitive. Growth isn't always straightforward and upwards, it can go sideways and downwards too. Growth twists and turns and sometimes snags and gnarls, it leaves you at times broken and battered, but as I told you at the very beginning, your roots will always sustain you.

It is true that more people are receiving treatment for mental health related issues than ever before. I say it again, it's ok not to be ok. It's ok to ask for help and receive help. This doesn't make you weak. It makes you strong. Six years ago my beautiful beloved niece Grace left this world. It was too soon. Grace was the most beautiful, sensitive, kind, artistic, generous soul you could ever meet. In school, Grace began to struggle with anxiety and was sensitive to the highs and lows of friendships. Her worries were exacerbated when she was bullied in her teens, excluded and ignored by former friends, pushed out and labelled annoying. This experience cut her deeply and, although she had done nothing wrong, she believed it was her fault and she began to protect herself in social groups by staying silent and not being herself. Just shy of her 19th birthday Grace left us when she took her own life. Sadly Grace never got the help she so desperately needed and she died in April 2018. She was in a coma for eight days but the damage was permanent and Gracie never regained consciousness. It was devastating. A light went out and though our family will never be the same again, Grace will live on for others. I am so proud of Grace's amazing mother. My sister-in-law, Ruth, has set up 'Grace To Restore', a charity to help young women have emotional stability and a mind free from distress, to give them the tools to live whole. To help young women with dark thoughts and destructive patterns of behaviour; self-harm and/or suicide ideation.

Grace needed support and help to recover from having become completely overwhelmed by life. Grace needed people alongside her to help her through the terrible darkness and anguish in her thoughts, to explain she wasn't going mad, but that she had an illness that she had every right to seek treatment for, not to feel ashamed of and as though she were a failure. There is always help and there is always hope. We all need it at some point in our lives. Don't be afraid to ask.

"When you judge yourself for needing help, you judge those you are helping. When you attach value to giving help, you attach value to needing help. The danger of tying your self-worth to being a helper is feeling shame when you have to ask for help. Offering help is courageous and compassionate, but so is asking for help."

Brené Brown, Rising Strong: The Reckoning. The Rumble. The Revolution.

We all need help sometimes. Financial, spiritual, emotional, and physical help are all things we may understandably need to simply get through life. It's a sad irony that it's during the times we most need to ask for help that most people are reticent in doing so. We have a fear of appearing too much or too needy. Fear of imposing, fear of revealing our struggle and having people realise we don't have it all together after all. Asking for help can cause feelings of uneasiness because we are essentially relinquishing control to someone else. But the truth is that going for help isn't a weakness but a strength. People want to be needed, to be asked, to help. Would you not want to extend help to someone that needed it? So be brave and extend that kindness to yourself and ask for help if you need it. Asking isn't taking, it is giving – giving someone else the opportunity to be strengthened and empowered by helping. Everyone is fighting a battle you don't know about, so be kind to them but be even kinder to yourself.

21
CURTAINS

Γίναμε μαλλιά κουβάρια.
We've become yarn balls.

Curtains is a medium-long fringed hairstyle, that mimics the look of curtains in the way that it hangs down both sides of the face, framing it. It's thought that curtain hair originated from the early 1900s, taking the place of the long hair and sideburns that were fashionable earlier during the late 1800s. Curtains proved to be a shorter alternative that was also more practical, as most men to adopt the trend were of the working class or played sports like rugby where long hair was impractical. Curtain hair made a revival in the '70s and then again in the '90s. Curtains made a comeback thanks to many male celebrities adopting the trend. Most notably, members of the Backstreet Boys, Tom Cruise, and Keanu Reeves also and perhaps less excitingly, my postman.

The word Curtains is also a slang expression referring to the end, ruin, or death of something. In the context of theatre, the singular term curtain has several specific uses. The literal curtain on a stage is used to conceal the stage until the performance is ready to be seen. Another sense of the word refers to when the curtain closes.

This can be a good thing. Whenever things come to an end it means a new beginning is in sight. The end of things is always better than the beginning. We're often told that all good things come to an end. But actually I think it is also true that some good things need to end in order for even better things to come. Find the treasure in the ending, as much as you do the new beginning.

"It is always important to know when something has reached its end. Closing circles, shutting doors, finishing chapters, it doesn't matter what we call it; what matters is to leave in the past those moments in life that are over."

Paulo Coelho

133

When I look back at my own life there are situations, personal and work-related, which I thought would be the end of me when they themselves ended. I thought I would be left wandering around lost in an abyss, without a reason to go on. As a child, I was frightened of endings most of all. The endings of movies, or books, or days out. I always feared the end of the day and having to go to sleep. Sleep terrified me even worse because it would usher in a new day of school. So I would often stay awake to stave off the morning. I always dreaded the ending of an event or family parties when it was time to go home. Anything that heralded the return to normal life filled me with fear. This terror always seemed to emerge from patterns that I couldn't understand. As a result, endings to me felt like some sort of punishment, so I learned to develop an irrational expectation of the end. Endings would come anyway, so sooner or later, my worst assumptions about myself and the world around me would always be proven true.

Understanding how we navigate processing and finding hope in an ending when we are experiencing loss is one of the hardest things. Coping with the loss of someone or something you love is one of life's most unfortunate and deeply sorrowful filled challenges.

My Mama would tell us the story of how she lost her youngest brother Yiannaki in 1964 when he was just 17 during the war in Cyprus. They carried him back to my grandmother's home and laid his bloody, lifeless body before her on the front porch. To this day he is a hero honoured with a statue in the village centre. He gave his life for his country, he risked everything to protect and rescue others, for which the family are incredibly proud. But the pain of searing loss was unspeakable. It altered my Mama and her loved ones, forever.

There is nothing more powerful than the coming together of great love and huge grief. I experienced those contrasting feelings at the time of my Baba's death. I loved him yet mourned him at the same time. I was pregnant at the time with new life kicking on the inside of me standing over his open grave. I was told to hold back my tears by relatives who feared the unleashing of my sorrow would cause me to lose my baby. Whatever your loss, it's personal to you, so don't feel ashamed about how you feel, or believe that it's somehow only appropriate to grieve for certain things and not others. Loss is loss. Allow yourself to have your feelings, give yourself permission. When you're grieving, it's more important than ever to take care of yourself. The stress of a major loss can quickly deplete your energy and emotional reserves. Looking after your physical and emotional needs will help you get through this difficult time.

Above all, face your feelings. You can try to suppress your grief, but you can't avoid it forever. In order to heal, you have to acknowledge the pain. Trying to avoid feelings of sadness and loss only prolongs the grieving process.

Without death there is no life. We don't need to fear it. The endings of things are sometimes better than the beginning. Endings are sobering, refining and can bring a beautiful light and clarity to a person. We don't need to be afraid of the endings but rather see them as an opportunity for new beginnings. We all need endings in order to have renewal and energy. Without winter there is no spring. As the daily, monthly, and yearly cycles change, everything in nature changes, too. Leaves change their colour, flowers turn into fruits, some animals sleep throughout the whole winter, and when they wake up, it's spring again and a new beginning.

We as humans, on the other hand, are obsessed with clinging to things. We want what we want now. We want to stay young forever. We find it difficult to embrace change maybe because this is a reminder that everything is transient. Accepting endings makes us more adaptable and that sets us free. I know there have been many disappointments and closed doors in my life that actually needed to happen. At the time though I was devastated. There were moments I was so close to getting my television series made, or people who I thought were for me suddenly changed and disappeared out of my life. You can experience numerous seasons over your lifetime – multiple springs, summers, autumns and winters. Changes in seasons give us permission to stop and bed down. I've learnt to be less afraid of things ending and seasons of change. Times of transition offer us the chance to establish new beginnings or to let go of old rhythms that will not serve us well once we are fully embedded in the coming new season. Without winter there is no spring.

♫

"Everything is everything
What is meant to be, will be
After winter, must come spring
Change, it comes eventually"

Lauryn Hill – Everything Is Everything

Endings are powerful and significant. Don't be in a hurry to run away from them. Stay with them and cherish them as you would your beginnings. Endings are painful, and the human tendency is to often personalise them as though we did something to deserve this. The fear of being alone, of being left or abandoned, is one of our deepest, most primal fears. Endings are part of life, and they can be a necessary part of the process and our own development. Endings can teach us to appreciate the present, and the people within it. There is nothing to fear, endings often show us a secret blessing or a good in the world we could never have seen without it. When something ends, allow yourself all the time and all the feelings; but then allow yourself, kindly and ever so gently in time, to move on when you are ready. Know this, every time your life stops or changes, you are about to start a new chapter.

22

DEEP CONDITIONING

Πέφτω από τα σύννεφα.
I fall from the clouds.

Deep conditioning is a procedure by which your hair is coated and treated with nourishing products. It restores your hair's moisture, strengthens it and reduces the damage caused to it by chemicals and styling products. It helps to define hair texture, seal ends and support healthy hair growth. Hair conditioner goes beneath the surface, put it this way it goes deep.

Once a week I like to give my own hair a deep conditioning treatment. I remember seeing my Mama do this in the shop. She would slather the customers hair with a thick blue conditioning mask and put them under the steamer, which was a funny looking contraption, it looked like a helmet stuck on a metal tripod with wheels. It was reinforced with elastic and a pair of old tights to keep it together. My Mama would turn the huge black clicky dial and the hot steam would come pouring out. The heat would accelerate the absorption process to make the customers hair silkier and softer.

Reflected in life too, metaphorically, conditioning is a deep process that changes your innermost being. It alters your response to situations. Conditioning is the process of training a person to respond to a stimulus in a certain way, by repeatedly exposing the person to a stimulus until they behave in the desired manner.

The situations I have been through in life have changed and conditioned me. Difficult struggles have forced me to confront my fears and overcome my obstacles, ultimately making me stronger both mentally and emotionally. It is through these adversities that we all develop important life skills that help make us more equipped to face the future.

Going through painful experiences change you, they alter you forever. The way I see the world, the way I receive people is so very different now to how I used to before I had my breakdown. I'm softer and gentler with myself and with others too. I used to be angry at myself when I made mistakes and would treat other people like this too when they made mistakes. I strove for perfection and expected to see it reflecting back at me through the actions of others. It's an exhausting way to live. I've had to set down the pain that was making me behave in this way. Now that I've let go of what I thought my life should look like, I feel free to enjoy the gift that it is now. I used to lament having lost years of my life of not making it as a performer sooner. But I know now this was all part of God's plan for me. Life for me has been in seasons. I sometimes feel a bit like Sarah in the Bible who struggled to conceive but finally got pregnant at 90. Sarah received the miracle of being able to conceive a child in her old age, and she bore Abraham a son of promise, Isaac. She became the mother of many nations and the mother of a royal line of kings. Her moment must have felt like a long time coming. She scoffed when God told her of the promise to come. I'm a bit like that, like seriously now that I'm firmly cemented in midlife, when I feel like a washed up old tea towel, are things happening for me? Are you sure you got this right God? Am I not way past it? Surely it's far too late. I wonder if you have ever felt that? Dismissed an opportunity because you thought it was too late for you.

I asked my Mama once whether looking back at her life she would have changed anything or whether she wished anything had been easier for her. Surprisingly she answered no. She said that even though she struggled greatly she accepted how things were. Her own Mama had shown her how to be content in the good and the bad. She said she never complained or wished the painful things away. She taught herself to endure them. She found a way to be happy wherever she was and with whatever was happening around her. She never wanted to be anywhere else other than the moment she was in. This she said made it all bearable. Even at the darkest of times she taught herself to be quiet and content. I then asked her where she found this happiness? I wanted to know how and where, in the pain, backbreaking hard work, and sacrifice she endured when we were little, she sourced this joy. "Olga," she said to me in her broken English "real happiness is the very little, little things, not big things. You can miss it. Is not money or the nice things. It's always right in front of you. Open your eyes."

When I look back at photos of myself as a young performer I see such excitement and wonder in my eyes. I wanted to be a famous theatre actress, so full of hopes and dreams. But life didn't go the way I planned it. I didn't become that famous actress but instead at 26 I decided I wanted to go out and teach drama in schools and orphanages in the Middle East. It's not where I thought I would end up but it was the turning point of my life and it fulfilled me in ways I never knew I needed. What's more, I met my husband out there. He was the love of my life. Then when I moved back to the U.K. I went on to have three sons who are my life's joy. At this point in my life I was knee deep in nappies, mashed broccoli and the stage became a distant memory. Later when the boys were all at school I studied to become a drama lecturer. I loved teaching young people performance. But deep down I still ached to do it myself. When I look back at photos of myself as a young actress I was so young and naive to think I could map it all out and life would just thank me for the blueprint and fall obediently into place.

I struggled for many years and found myself missing, as a woman and as a mother. I didn't recognise my own reflection in the mirror. I looked like a ghost, a shadow. I felt buried, forgotten by others and even worse by myself. I felt like dying, but I didn't. I held on. I fought, allowing the tent corners of my existence to be stretched and lengthened. My insides were tested, pulled, stretched. I became steadfast and resilient. Nothing else could ever terrify me again. Fire tests the purity of gold, when impurities are burned away, the remaining gold is 24 carat and considered very valuable. So too trials refine and test us making us stronger, unshakeable, both in body and mind. As I entered my forties light came flooding back in again and I reconnected with that young woman in the photos. After my breakdown I realised there was nothing left to be afraid of anymore. I saw my demons and as ugly as they were, they were powerless; if I poked my finger into them they vanished, disappeared like a puff of smoke. I remembered that young actress and how excited she was about life. I came back to her. I came back to myself and back to my dreams. I began to sing again and the song sounded sweeter, fuller, richer. I allowed myself to smile and hope again, my mouth filled with laughter and I was able to sleep soundly and enjoy my food again. I found myself and step by step, made my way back to the stage.

A lot of the content and writing I create is a comedic reimagining of the trauma I faced as a bullied immigrant Cypriot kid. The anger of those early years in my life got repressed, shoved down. I didn't know what to do with it and where to put it. I remember coming home every day after school, screaming into my pillow. In rage I jabbed my arms with pencils. But what if I had taken my revenge out on those bullies and not myself. That bottled rage manifested itself in low self-esteem and depression and later in the form of my breakdown. I fell apart, but it led to me finding my comedic voice and rebuilding myself through laughter. That assault of trauma though it brought me to my knees had also bedded me down and shaped me, making me who I am today. I really wouldn't have had it any other way. This was my tempering, my softening, my deep conditioning. My content has always been an expression of both comedy and sadness, both have always co-existed side by side in my life and in my work. Taking revenge on those who had hurt me I believe would never have given me satisfaction. It would have destroyed me. I learnt how to gather myself with dignity, to rise and to forgive. I found power in meekness and strength in the waiting.

I have always carried the hope that all things work together for good. Nothing, no matter how small, is ever wasted. My life is more beautiful because of everything I have been through. All the rich layers fall together, cascading down into one beautiful, bounteous hairstyle if you like. For all the pain I've been through in my life I would not change a thing. I have always chosen love. To repay wickedness with kindness. I am who I am because of the road I have walked and I wouldn't trade it for anything. I have more compassion and forbearance for others. I think I'm more skilled as a writer and stronger as a performer because of everything I have been through. I can see how my talent has been honed, seasoned, sharpened. I now have the maturity and strength of character to withstand. It was always going to be this way.

"Sometimes when you're in a dark place you think you've been buried, but you've actually been planted."

Christine Caine

The events of the past do not determine your future, but rather they have made you stronger to face it. Instead of dwelling on negative situations, see them as a way to propel you forward. Sometimes, to heal, you first need to allow yourself to feel. Bottling up your thoughts and emotions may hurt you more in the long run. Think of how strong these past hurts have made you. Think about the amazing coping skills you developed and who was there for you when you were struggling. Ruminating on 'what if's and 'should have's will stop you moving forward. Rather, being brave and openly expressing how you feel, will help you to feel grounded and make room for new experiences. By focusing on the lessons you learned and the gold you unearthed within yourself you can gently let go of emotional pain and bravely move forward.

23

EXTENSIONS

Κάλλιο αργά παρά ποτέ.
Better late than never.

Artificial hair integrations, more commonly known as hair extensions or hair weaves, are usually clipped, glued, or sewn onto natural hair, incorporating additional human or synthetic hair. You can find some truly hideous hair extensions online that can make you look like you have a small, rabid squirrel attached to your head. It's tragic, but sometimes you can't get away from the fact that bad hair extensions happen to good people. In general you can think of an extension being a part that is added to something to enlarge or prolong it. I feel like getting older is my personal extension, that midlife has become my unexpected stage, my wonderful add on. Getting older can be a pain in the ass, literally, not to mention your knees, back, shoulders, shall I go on? But it's also full of rich and wonderful unexpected additions. A bit like having two naan breads delivered in your takeaway when you only ordered and paid for one. I'm embracing midlife as my little something extra and unexpected. I'm settling in and enjoying all the comedy potential I can wring out of my midlife waterproof bib. It's easy to get older and think, now what? Where does life leave me now? Where do I go from here? I'm right here living my best hot-flushing, mash-potato-brained, menopausal life, slap bang facing fifty and I'm damn well going to make comedy about the heart palpitating, here and now of it.

Personally, I refuse to pump myself with cow offering botox products to look younger. Disclaimer: I would feed them to my kids without question from the frozen fast food section as it appears this is the kind of dubious fare they enjoy. I don't want to eradicate the lines on my face, all the little marks that etch my life's story.

"That's another great thing about getting older. Your life is written on your face."

Frances McDormand

As an actor I want my face to be able to move and express itself when I'm on stage. Olga is getting on a bit now and hot damn she may as well have some – losing her marbles – fun with it.

I've accepted that I'm rapidly turning into my Mama and there's nothing I can do about it, so I may as well laugh about it and accept it. For example, the other day I chased my neighbour down the road to feed him a pizza. I keep saying "Are you hungry?" like a nervous tick. It's like a knee jerk response to any problem. I once said "I love you" to the builder by mistake? Tell me this has happened to us all? That and calling your bank manager honey boo boo. No problem, eat something! You've only got £8.57 to last you till the end of the month and it's only the 6th? No problem, just eat something! It's the Grecian way my friend. Listen, if I can't solve a problem I'm just gonna throw food at it. By the way, are you hungry? You sure? Maybe I should have given away a vat of hummus and a giant koulouri baton with every copy of this book. I know, I know I'm being ridiculous, that'll be for book number two.

Growing up as a kid my Mama would always use old margarine tubs to store food in. The alluring Roses tin always deceivingly harboured stewed pigs' brains in it. I remember opening the metal tin once to take a chocolate only to be greeted by a pig's snout swimming in gelatin. FYI for the record, (understandably) I'm a veggie now. But in a cruel twist of fate I do this very same unhinged thing to my own kids. The sexy ice cream tub (the one that rhymes with Glenn and Sherrys) is falsely beguiling to them as I use it to store leftover shepherd's pie. I'd be lying if I said I didn't find the disappointment on their faces at the sight of frozen mince amusing. Come on there have to be SOME perks to motherhood.

In addition to the compulsive feeding up of strangers, most tragically I've discovered that I'm getting random hairs EVERYWHERE. I must confess to you that there is a recurring one on my chest which is so familiar to me now I feel like it would be rude not to name him. Yes, the offending article is most definitely masculine, I'm telling you hands down it's a 'he' for sure. I'm thinking Keith would be a good name.

Furthermore in this delightful new phase of life I've started taking a cardigan out with me wherever I go just in case. I have officially entered 'cardi-gate'. What do you expect? I mean I'm not going to live dangerously on the edge, have you seen the erratic UK weather? Why chance it? Also I've started popping in an extra pair of knickers in my handbag for good measure. Always be prepared to be knocked down by a fast moving vehicle and rushed to hospital, or for Gerard Butler to spot you in Aldi's middle aisle and sweep you off your feet to the local Travelodge for a wild night of takeaway ordering and watching QVC. Or maybe just keep a pair in case you wet yourself. I've even started making these deep appreciative noises whenever I sit down; not unlike those made by horses. It's now mandatory that I must always put my pyjamas on by 5pm. Also I repeat myself. I repeat myself. I repeat myself. I think you get the idea.

Yes I'm having a big fat Greek midlife crisis and I don't care who knows about it. I might even get it printed as my bumper sticker. MENOPAUSAL WOMAN ONBOARD. I want to get myself a giant Oodie, with huge handy pockets for my HRT medications and copious bags of Monster Munch. Casserole dishes now officially get my pulse racing. My husband still does too of course, but only when he isn't (A) noisily eating a Müller crunch corner or (B) cutting his toenails in front of me. I'm actually really not sure what's worse. Cooking pots, pans and serving dishes have now become an obsession for me, a sort of mature lady fetish. I think it began when as a chubby monobrowed 7-year-old I saw my Mama unwrap a saucepan set from Argos one Christmas from my Baba. I recall him calling her over to our '80s highly flammable balloon and tinsel covered tree and proudly presented her with the wrapped saucepans. "Nitsa I got a very big surprise for you ah. You are a VERY lucky woman! Is gonna change your life. Look ah, this is a big one!" I was sold. Seriously though, purchasing the right shape and the right make consumes me. It's my MLM: my middle-life mission. You see it's all about finding that one magical piece of cookware that will elevate me from a regular mum to a Nigella mum. So I bought the 'mack daddy' of all cookware, a sex hot Creuset. Be assured it's a very fancy pants piece of cookware. You know how women get push presents when they have a baby? (I'm still waiting for mine by the way, I'm hoping I'll receive some sort of bounty before they all fly the nest). Well this was my 'Menopausal womb is officially shut' present to myself. I wanted to be the kind of seasoned woman who could really handle one. I wanted to grip that middle class status bad boy in my Ikea panelled kitchen, and show him who was boss. I genuinely thought my life would change. A new dawn had come and I would be the kind of woman who cooked incredible Instagram worthy dishes for her adoring family. A wife of noble character whose husband and children arise and call her blessed among women and their inferior cookware. To be fair all I've ended up cooking is soul-killing mum bolognese that makes my kids gag, but hold up, I can justify it because it looks so good on the stove.

Another sign I'm having a midlife crisis is that without fail I do my towels on a Wednesday and my sheets on a Saturday. Any deviation is cause for alarm. Also I've developed this weird thing where I never leave knives out overnight on the kitchen counter. I mean who wants to make things easy for an axe murderer who might casually happen to break in in the middle of the night. You can't be too careful. Let me paint the scene for you. Enter the axe murderer, let's give them a balaclava for effect, and, purely for my amusement, bicycle clips on their trousers. "Oh look," they go, "here's a kitchen knife-slash-deadly killer weapon that's thrillingly tempting and handy." No way mate I say as I appear in the kitchen doorway, half-asleep, my hair on end, wearing my four cardigans, if you're going to break in and hack this menopausal body to pieces, bring your own utensils, oh alright just help yourself look in the top drawer. I don't mind leaving spoons out though, I can't see much that a bloodthirsty psychopath can do with that. Now tell me honestly is that a sign of a midlife crisis or the fact that I am just plain weird. Don't answer that.

Please don't get me started on the way I sleep these days, I'm talking ear plugs, eye masks and mouthguards. There's a whole midlife sleep narrative there for another whole book, the one I'm going to give that vat of hummus away with remember? My poor husband. I go to bed every night looking and sounding like Rocky Balboa. It's hard to say goodnight sexily whilst wearing a mouthguard. Have you tried it? I have this other thing that I must admit to you, I am obsessed with reading tedious Amazon reviews. I can't get enough, I'm insatiable. I read them ALL. I am truly stunned at the depths of sheer stupidity to which mankind has fallen. Amazon reviews are like a fatal car crash. You try really hard not to look but you can't help yourself. Cue Sue from Leighton Buzzard: "Can I also use this fountain pen as an eye liner?" No you can't Sue, you lunatic! The other day I got lost in the dark underbelly of Amazon reviews investigating hard foot skin scrapers with a legit actual person, Barry From Birmingham asking "Could this hard skin foot scraper be used for grating parmesan cheese?" Disturbing, does Barry ever wonder why nobody wants to come over for dinner? You would be surprised at the amount of alliteration you can find on Amazon reviews. Rita from Roehampton, Derek from Dundee. Crystal from Crewe. I know because I told you I read them all. I have no life.

Olga is getting older. Hell yeah, I'm going to capitalise it. OLGA IS GETTING OLDER. Darn it I forgot to put it in bold font. Look, quite frankly I've considered it; putting myself in the freezer so I can stay young and desirable but I can't because A) I can't find a freezer big enough, B) I don't like the cold and C) I'm actually excited to get older. I hate the whole, 'you look good for your age'. I hate that. What does it even mean? Just tell me I look good full stop. Also it would be lovely to be fancied by strangers. There I said it. I want to be fancied, desperately, to be honest who doesn't. No, I'm sorry, my husband does not count, he has to fancy me; and no not the 70-year-old Tesco delivery driver, think casanova with no teeth, who always asks for my number when he delivers my groceries.

Yet another sign I'm getting to "that" stage of life is that though my libido has most definitely left the building, weirdly I'm lusting after younger men. A few months ago the plumber came round and I was naturally expecting the usual fare that comes knocking at your door. Ordinarily the kind of tradesmen I get turning up look like Shrek or Keith Chegwin. But this one was B-A-eautiful, a dead ringer for a young David Beckham. I was beside myself and my body lost complete control. Picture the scene, my full on double chins trembling, my pits moist, I was dribbling, a bit of wee came out. I had it ALL going on. The poor guy was probably looking at me thinking that I was just a nice lady, like his mum. Ouch. I was genuinely taken aback at the wrench wielding, bicep bulging, tanned stallion at my door. Also, I noticed his hands were beautifully smooth and manicured which made me question whether he was in fact a plumber at all and perhaps just a kiss-o-gram sent as an early 50th present by one of my girlfriends. But alas no. Not that I'm suggesting plumbers are unattractive for the most part. (Well I sort of am). He was so lovely to look at and brightened up my wet Monday so much that with wild abandon I gave him freshly brewed coffee, not the instant rubbish I give to the Keith Chegwin rabble. Unfortunately though, it seems the only men who seem to fancy me these days are large, unattractive bald businessmen with briefcases, eating breakfasts in Premier Inns. True story.

Yes reader I, Olga Thompson, have finally been summoned by the death knell of female midlife. That hot-flushing, irregular-bleeding, irritable, bloated elephant in the room. The 'M' word. The unmentionable 'ladies' modern day plague. Menopause baby! I am firmly cemented in the bulging Aldi middle aisle section of life. I am getting older and softer around the edges now, my waist is thicker and my boobs have fallen out with each other and gone their separate ways. Also I suspect that I'm shrinking, which at 5ft nothing isn't thrilling news. Recently my boys told me they were adamant that I was now 4ft 10 which meant I could be legitimately categorized as a dwarf. When I spoke to my doctor about all my menopausal symptoms she told me to look on the bright side, because it was better than the alternative. Let me unpack it for you: she meant I could be dead. Sobering. But I may as well be because sometimes as an older woman I'm made to feel like I don't exist. I'm not visible. Society favours the young and the beautiful without hormonal malfunctions and leaky bowel issues. But one day those young and beautiful people will have hormonal malfunctions and leaky bowel issues too. And I will be right here delightedly waiting for them with a giant Tena lady pad. I will never be so cruel as to say I told you so, no, I will just think it instead, as I sit a grey old lady, long hair down to my bum crack, crocheting tea cosies and rocking by the fire as I wait for devilishly good-looking plumbers to arrive at my lair. One day all of these now young people will have jowelage and turkey necks like me. I'm rocking both and loving it. You'll find me right here cheering and sticking out my Turkey neck and paving the way ahead for all the younger women behind me. I will no longer be invisible with my grand master plan. Oh yes, I'm going to rename myself My Big Fat Greek Saggy Tits; yeah that oughta do it.

Something happened to me as I hit my forties. I stopped caring about little things like Julie giving me a funny look on the school run. Sorry if you're reading this and your name is in fact Julie it's not personal. I think Julie is a lovely name. I could have chosen Karen or Sharon or Bev. Look, I have got far more important things to worry about now than caring about everyone's personal opinion of me. I'm far too busy reading moronic Amazon reviews and letching after embryonic tradesmen. I don't have time to people please anymore. I can't make everyone happy. I grew up thinking people only liked me if I kept them laughing. The chubby hairy, immigrant Greek kid, who did funny skits for the other kids in the playground so she wouldn't get bullied. Olga Thompson is just not that girl anymore. Do one Julie.

Menopause has given me a mahoosive kick up the behind. I've had to shape up and look after myself a lot more. To try and do one little thing for myself, that isn't working or cleaning the house or ferrying boys or nipping to yet another supermarket for tortoise food, Lynx black and bananas. Why is it always the bananas that need topping up in my house? I often wonder if I'm living with chimps. I've actually taken to heaving my weary mum bod into a barely worn swimsuit and braved my local leisure centre pool. I've even endured the lengthy two hour shave it takes to de-fuzz my hairy legs. Alas, my Lady Garden is frightfully overgrown and shall require lengthy industrial action at a much later date. Probably never. Yes I feel uncomfortable walking out to the pool in a swimsuit, not unlike my 10-year-old self back in the days of the grotty school swim sessions at Arnos Grove pool where the boys laughed at my stubby furry legs and I witnessed a floating turd.

Have I made you laugh? There you go. You see I told you, midlife is my extension, my unexpected appendage! It's my new found place and I really, really love it. We have to keep laughing and celebrating who we are, because ageing is actually brilliant! It ushers you into new uncharted territory where you can get away with everything by pretending to be that mad old lady eating out of a Cheerios packet in the supermarket. My favourite pastime is telling cold callers I'm not sure what to do with my husband's dead body. Try it, I promise you they will never call back. Sure I'm not 35 anymore, but I'm not a Golden Girl yet either. Bagsy I'm Blanche by the way because well, quite frankly, she was my favourite. I have been bruised and battered by life, but the blueprint of who I am on the inside is unchanged. I'm still that young girl inside, I'm still just a big kid at heart. I promised myself after my breakdown that I wouldn't hide anymore. See me, here is my story. I am older, yes, but only now do I feel complete.

There will be many women reading this book who feel just like me. I see you and I feel, just like you, hot, flustered and forgotten. We are what they annoyingly call 'women of a certain age'. I detest this phrase as much as I detest the odious manager in my local Holland and Barrett who referred to me in that way. I what-in-the-herbal-holistic-stratosphere kid you not. Maybe it was my foldaway shopper that gave me away at the time I don't know but those were the words he uttered. "Excuse me madam, are you perhaps looking for something for women of a certain age?" Ooh I don't know a hacksaw perhaps to cut your "supplements" off?. I will forever regret not responding with those words. Flummoxed I told him I was only 37, hastily grabbing a vat of primrose oil and sharply exiting out.

Sometimes I want to bury my head in my hands and weep at the way middle aged women are perceived. But I refuse to. I'm set on creating comedy that keeps women like myself laughing and celebrating who we are now. I refuse to stay silent as I sit here in my Tena lady pants. No, I want you all to flippin' well know about it. I'm not clapped out and redundant because I'm over 40. I had to put my big fat Greek girl pants on when I was approached to write a book about my life because, quite frankly, I wanted to run for the hills. Why would anyone want to read this, the voice in my head said. Who are you? You are too old now surely? What on earth are you going to say? Well from the volume of words in this book quite a lot it seems. I had to push hard to write this book because I knew I wasn't writing it just for myself. The honest truth is I wrote it for you too. For all of us women of a certain age. Make room for us, we aren't dead yet. In fact we are only just getting started.

"Getting older makes you more alive. More vitality, more interest, more intelligence, more grace, more expansion."

Jamie Lee Curtis

We all get sucked into messages that tell us ageing is something we are supposed to dread or incessantly lament. Getting older is not the end. It is so stunningly humbling and hugely awe-inspiring to be alive every single day. No you are not too old and no it is not too late. Who told you this rubbish? You have grandmas getting their master's degrees at 85! There's no expiration date on our ambitions, nor any predetermined age by which a particular goal must be reached. There are so many famous people who didn't make it till they were 40. You are not too old to change your life, to ditch negative thinking and overcome obstacles. Set everything that hinders you aside and hot foot it towards what you still can and will become. Can I get an Amen? Your girl just PREACHED!

24

SWEEPING UP

Μαλλιασε η γλώσσα μου
My tongue has grown hair.

We all want to look good and feel our best don't we? But finding the time and motivation to care for ourselves can be challenging. One simple easy way to look and feel great is by getting a haircut right? Also eating a box of Ferrero Rochers in one sitting can also give you a little pick me up. Monsieur, you're really spoiling us. But seriously, taking care of our appearance helps us feel better about ourselves and reduces anxiety and stress levels. Basically when we look good, we feel good. What joy there is to be found at the salon, an undisturbed cup of tea, browsing a magazine in peace, a relaxing hair wash, no one to ask me what's for dinner. Right, I'm off to the hairdressers.

I'm always re-energised after a trip to the salon, my hair sort of sprightly bounces behind me as I merrily skip out and down the street. I feel ready to take on the world even though, more often than not, I'm just going home to make sausage and mash.

Mama would always say that if she dropped the comb when she was cutting a customer's hair it meant good luck, a fortuitous omen. It meant that the customers' hair would turn out beautifully. I remember her saying "Oh Jean you so lucky I drop my comb, your hair is gonna be nice today". One of my jobs in the salon was sweeping up all the cut hair off the salon floor. I loved looking at all the hair clippings smattered all over the worn green lino, all the different strands and colours from all the different customers, all amassed and woven together like an abstract tapestry.

Cutting one's hair can be cathartic, almost ritualistic, where the bad things are cut away. A kind of shedding almost, like a caterpillar outgrowing and wriggling out of its tight, old skin. The caterpillar is completely lost, replaced by something far more beautiful that has been forged in loss, struggle, and potentially pain. Everything that has been cut away comes back more magnificent, more glorious when it becomes a butterfly. For many shrubs, the purpose of cutting and pruning is to remove old, dead and crossing shoots, as well as those that produced flowers. This encourages the development of fresh shoots to grow and thrive. Pruning and shedding is a necessary and fundamental part of nature. Gardeners prune plants to encourage growth and improve plant health. Dead or dying plant parts are not only unattractive but also harmful to the plant. Pruning is a powerful metaphor that describes the process of removing things that hinder growth, whether that's in a spiritual, personal, or psychological sense. There is a time for death and a time for birth. A time to be planted and a time to uproot. Things end and they begin again. This is the natural flow of things, the order of life.

> **There is a time for everything, and a season for every activity under the heavens: a time to be born and a time to die, a time to plant and a time to uproot.**
>
> Ecclesiastes 3:1-2 (NIV)

After my breakdown, the old dead ways of thinking about myself felt like they were cut away. In many ways I felt new, raw, reborn. I could see the hopeful little green shoots that I had waited for for so long finally coming through the dry parched landscape of my existence. As I stand over the cuttings of my life, the smattering of hair clippings on the floor, the split ends and the dead ends, I sense a huge unburdening, a massive sense of relief.

A weight has lifted, the tension my tired body has wearily carried for years dissipates and dissolves. I can breathe deeply again. I can see a shedding has taken place of all the old ways of thinking and being, ushering in a new beginning. I am lighter. The world feels lighter, the air itself has changed, no longer full of dread and fear. My chest expands and for the first time in what feels like forever, my mind is quiet. And in that stillness, there is space and room for hope to live again. Relief is not a grand gesture, but a soft shift, like the slow turning of a page or the softening of a familiar ache. It's the return of peace, unnoticed at first, until you realize you've been living without it for far too long.

When something new is happening, you need to make room for it. It may mean letting go of the things that no longer serve you in order for you to grow. The cutting and pruning of self, the shedding of tired habits, have all helped me to change for the better. What I have been through has been a necessary means to this end. Pruning can often feel counterintuitive. We see growth as a sign of success and health, so why would we ever want to cut it off? Why would I want to cut my hair when I'm desperately trying to grow it long? But cutting away leads to regeneration and regrowth. The joy of what I found ahead was so much greater than what I had left behind. It came to a point where I stopped fighting for what I thought my life should look like, instead I surrendered to what it was.

I had spent so long feeling afraid. Wanting to give up, to hide, to run away, to avoid. I felt drained from trying to control outcomes that simply could not be controlled. I was battling overwhelming past trauma and exhausted from fighting stark reality. So I allowed myself to stand still and shed. The delicate layers of my past self, the remnants of how I endured, fell from me. I found that when I surrendered I was able to accept the situations that were happening and make peace with them. I came home to myself. I felt released from the need to have all of the answers. The dross, the dead ends of my life fell away from me. I felt lighter and freer. I've finally stepped into the person I was always meant to be and left the past behind. I've embraced my life and given myself the permission I so needed to live it. Surrendering has helped me to see what I've been tripping over my whole life. I've gone back to that little girl who did crazy shows for her family in the living room and sang in the mirror with her hair brush. I live with a carefree abandon now, knowing that it's ok not to be ok. I don't need to have all the answers. I can be spontaneous and allow life to just happen to me, rather than trying to harness and control it like a wild animal.

Surrendering for me has been a long process. It wasn't overnight. It wasn't something I announced. I quietly let go of the need to fight against the current. I stopped wrestling with the tide and made peace with it, I had nothing left in me to attempt to try and swim against it. My resources were depleted, it was futile. In surrender, there is a wondrous paradox: strength in yielding, wisdom in silence, freedom in letting go. I used to suffer debilitating panic attacks when I couldn't see my way out of things. Now I've learnt to be patient and sit with the discomfort, eventually the exit sign makes itself known. When I make myself calm and still I always find the way out.

My life like most people's hasn't been linear and unproblematic, it's been winding and complicated. Every time I thought I knew which way to go, suddenly I was redirected to somewhere else. I know I'm now walking on a different road to the one I intended. My dead ends led me to unexpected detours which led me to unearth so much unexpected treasure. Performing on platforms and stages I never imagined and I'm welcoming it, all of it, exactly as it comes. I'm no longer trying to advance with massive strides, I'm taking one little step at a time.

Now that I've given myself permission to just be, I feel freer, I'm more creative and I definitely think (hope) I'm funnier. People even tell me I look different now, contented, calmer and more relaxed and that makes me so very happy to hear. I'm grateful for everything I've overcome. Cutaway are the years, failures, indecisions, losses, unhealthy attachments, uncertainty, regrets, doubts and negativity that I've chosen to let go. I've stopped identifying myself as those dead things.

Interestingly, my relationship with my hair also taught me important life lessons of learning how to let go. By choosing to allow my hair the freedom to do its own thing, it's made me let go, breathe and relinquish control a lot more too. It turns out, when you surrender, amazing things happen. I have developed a daily habit of saying "I surrender" to my creator, each day I am ready to start over. My perspective has changed, I am not the bad things that happened to me. I choose to live in the now. I choose to live authentically. I'm not afraid to be vulnerable and to say to the world, "I am alive." I no longer hide. The term "authentic" originates from the Greek word "authentikos" (αύθεντικός), which means 'original' or 'principal'. I love that. We are all original works baby, every single one of us.

I've allowed myself to take my space in this world. I no longer have to make myself small and neither do you. We think we have to choose to be less than our grandest version of ourselves. We think that if others hear our true voice, they won't listen and the disappointment we feel will be worse for it. But now, it's time to get loud. I've decided to take up the space that was always rightfully mine. At drama school we were taught as actors to 'take the space', that is to 'own' our ground. It wasn't necessarily an action but more of an inner feeling that swelled and grew in the actor's chest. It was an affirmative "Here I am, look at me I own the space I stand in". Please never ever apologise for who you are. Do you realise how insanely precious you are? Like really? Take up the space that is yours. I feel like I spent most of my life apologising and shoehorning myself into corners to please others. I am now literally allergic to letting others walk all over me anymore.

So if you feel you need to, then just surrender. Let it all go. We are forever spinning those plates aren't we? What if we let a couple drop? In the English language plate spinning is used as a metaphor; it describes a sort of juggling act where you keep as many plates spinning as you can on top of poles. If a plate stops spinning, it will fall and break so you have to visit each plate as it slows to speed it up again. This got me thinking. We try to keep so many plates spinning in our lives for fear of them falling to the ground and smashing into pieces. People plates, relationship plates, family plates, money plates, problem plates, work plates, friend plates. But we were never made to keep all the plates spinning at all times. Sometimes there are things, people and situations that you just need to let go of. Keeping all those plates spinning will drain you and leave you feeling fearful, exhausted and duty bound. Unfortunately some of those plates are just going to have to stop spinning, fall to the ground and smash. It's ok. Let them.

The origins of the Greek tradition of plate smashing started years ago in Greece when a rich family invited a much poorer family to dinner and to make them feel better, they invited them to break their plates. They were proving that we worry about so many unnecessary things, but love and friendship is everything. The voluntary breaking of plates, which is also a type of controlled loss in my culture, is also an act of celebration, of letting things go. So I invite you reading this to smash some plates with me. I am at a stage in my life where I realise I can't make everyone happy and that's more than okay. I feel relieved, joyous and excited about the breakages at my feet. Be brave and let those plates fall too; let go, rejoice and smash them to the ground. OPA! Your new chapter is coming. Now whack up Zorba the Greek, and come smash some plates with me.

Sometimes letting go is the most powerful thing you can do. We fear that if we let something go we will be left bereft, empty and at a loss with nothing to fill the chasm, but oftentimes the old needs to go, in order for the new to come. Sometimes letting go can look like choosing forgiveness, leaving a place of work, or releasing anxious feelings about ourselves. Whatever it is, be safe in the knowledge that you have outgrown it and it doesn't serve you anymore. If it's taking up your air, let it go so you can breathe again. Cutting things away can be painful but is necessary. Life has a way of presenting us with the same lessons until we learn them and when we do we experience a life changing shedding, a cropping, a release, a cathartic move forward.

One of my favourite shows on telly growing up was *Record Breakers* with Roy Castle. The premise of the series was to celebrate world record feats, whether great Olympic athletes or men who built models of the Titanic out of matches. The show theme song would go "dedication's what you need if you wanna be a record breaker." True grit is living life like it's a marathon, not a sprint. My most treasured Aesop fable is the one that tells of a race between a speedy hare and a slow tortoise. The overconfident hare takes a nap during the race, while the tortoise slowly but steadily advances to victory. The moral of the fable is "Plodding wins the race". I have taught myself not to stare at disappointment for too long, but to pick myself up and keep going. I've done the years of feeling sorry for myself. It doesn't get me anywhere and only wastes valuable time. Keep going no matter what. Never compromise and never lose sight of those dreams. Plod on baby.

My breakdown took me to a place where I was forced to let go of everything, but surrendering brought everything back together. My life has been a gift. So many times I look back and I'm so thankful that I never gave up. I'm Olga Thompson and I am a comedian but I've learnt it's also okay to drop the act. I don't need to hide anymore, I can stop putting on a mask and accept myself totally.

As I sweep up the split ends of my life so far, I see now that they themselves can be ever so beautiful. After all, without them being there as a reminder, you might overlook cutting your hair. A reminder of all the experiences I have overcome. My life has been like a sum of all the wondrous places I have been to and all the precious people I have known. Just like those collections of hair on El Greco's salon floor. A mixture of moments and sounds wonderfully complex, not orderly and in place but dishevelled and multilayered.

We build up our cities and countries on actual bricks and mortar, but we build our lives on what we have done and the wisdom gained from all our mistakes and our successes. As I close this book, as I hang up the wet towels on the indoor makeshift washing line, it's almost time to go home. I close the appointments book and turn the signage over from open to closed. As I sweep a mass of hair up I think about all the cuttings of my life, smatterings of conversations and experiences, of journeys and people. I think about how everything has come together, worked together for good. As I sweep up all the pieces of my life, all the fragments of past memories and dreams yet to be fulfilled, I see a softer kinder version of myself has emerged. I've chosen to love myself, to give myself permission. I've finally chosen to give myself a chance. Maybe when you finally put this book down, you could give yourself a chance too.

Try to be grateful everyday, it can help you feel better about your life. Being grateful is good for your soul and your health. Take the time to write down what you're grateful for each and every day, even if you start with the smallest of things. I know at my lowest points I've had to look back at how far I've come and give myself a pat on the back. I know there are some days where even this kind of thinking doesn't help, especially when we can be at our lowest, so I start with the little things. The breath in my lungs, the food on my table. I remind myself how far I have come. This always lifts me out of my slump. So live in the moment. You can't change the past and you have no control of the future so just enjoy what's in front of you right here, right now. When you're busy making too many plans, you can feel stressed and prevented from enjoying the present. Before I was wracked with fear over the future and haunted by the past but now I smile when I catch myself enjoying the moment. You and I don't need everything perfect and straight in order to live life. Go for it. Everything always works together for good. I promise you that.

EPILOGUE

Πάρε δρόμο
Take road.

Sometimes the very things we want to run from are actually the things sent to save us. I wish I'd known all those years ago as I sat watching my Mama finish women's hair in the hairdressing chair, as I sat watching the clock slowly and painstakingly tick by, that I was watching my life unfold. Those ordinary, dull mundane moments that seem insignificant at the time are the blank canvases onto which our lives are sketched. Everything comes full circle. We always carry within us the place where we began. Those mundane everyday little things become the greatest things. Treasure them and catch them before they disappear. Life is never something you wait for, it's always happening all the time, right there under your feet.

Thank you for reading this book. Thank you for taking a chance on that clumsy, repressed, chubby, scissor happy enthusiast who knows that good always overcomes the bad, that darkness gives way to light and that faithfulness always brings blessing. Thank you for taking a chance on the chubby, bushy browed, mullet-haired girl who home-waxed herself with sellotape behind her father's back. Thank you for taking a chance on me. That bullied, little immigrant girl who became an entertainer, mental health campaigner and spokeswoman for others. This is a story I've been wanting to tell all my life.

Thank you to my friends and family for all their support and encouragement. To my beautiful husband Paul, my whole life, my best friend, my fellow Elvis enthusiast and my rock, love you forever. Thank you my Paulie T for all the endless cups of tea and early morning standing in the kitchen in our pyjamas hugs. It was always meant to be you.

My darling boys Harrison, Marcus and Pierce for being such incredible, kind, thoughtful young men and for always believing in their crazy little Mimi. You make me so proud. This is all for you.

To the best hairdresser I know my wonderful Mama Helen. Mama mou thank you for all your sacrifices, for loving me and making me the woman I am today but above all thank you for giving me that unforgettable mullet. I couldn't have written this book without you.

Massive thanks to the most incredible publishing team at Synergy Publishing for supporting and believing in me. Special thank you to Cam Toman the creative director at Synergy, you have helped bring my story to life with your beautiful design. Thank you for listening and hearing my voice Cam. Suzi, thank you for asking me to write this book, I value your love, friendship and endless Whatsapp notes. Thank you all for being my wonderful book family, you are never getting rid of me now. Love you all.

Thank you to my amazingly talented Editor, Nicole for guiding and supporting me during the writing process with endless encouraging notes and messages and for just being my wonderful girl.

Biggest thanks to Katie and her fantastic team at Read Maxwell for encouraging me and helping to get the word out when quite frankly I wanted to hide inside my wheelie bin.

But above all I thank Father God for knowing me and restoring everything that was lost. For bringing new beginnings out of the split ends. Love you Abba.

And the LORD blessed the latter days of Job more than his beginning.

Job 42:12 (ESV)